The Unknown God

The Unknown God

Mark E. Petersen

Bookcraft, Inc., Salt Lake City, Utah

Library of Congress Catalog Card Number: 78-51567
ISBN O-88494-337-2

First Printing, 1978

Lithographed in the United States of America
PUBLISHERS PRESS
Salt Lake City, Utah

BEHOLD,

I am Jesus Christ,

whom the prophets testified shall come into the world.

And behold, I am the light and the life of the world; and I have drunk out of that bitter cup which the Father hath given me, and have glorified the Father in taking upon me the sins of the world, in the which I have suffered the will of the Father in all things from the beginning.

— 3 Nephi 11:10 - 11

I AM the first and the last;
I AM he who liveth,
I AM he who was slain;
I AM your advocate with the Father.

— D&C 110:4

Contents

Chapter One

Fun and More Fun

What do people want most in life? Also, <u>what is our greatest need?</u> They are two different things.

It seems that above everything else the majority wants to have a continuous good time and, of course, the leisure and money to go with it.

But our overwhelming need is something else. It is always with us. It won't go away. It is like a shadow and follows us wherever we go. We often allow our overriding desires to dwarf it, but this we can never fully do.

And what is that need? <u>It is an understanding of God! It is a realization of how the Almighty relates to our personal lives. Such an understanding would be our beacon to success and stability.</u>

To most people the Deity is an unknown. A recent Gallup poll showed that 90 percent of all Americans believe there is a God, but few of them have any sound idea of what or who he is.

Nearly half (44 percent) of all Americans go to Church every Sunday, and this is wonderful compared to the 3 to 4 percent on the continent of Europe, and the 5 to 10 percent in Great Britain. But even as they worship they are not sure about the object of their adoration — what he is, what he can do for them, or what claim he has to their allegiance. Everyone needs to *know!*

Recreation has the center of the stage in America just now. Last year we spent 160 billion dollars on it, which is three times the cost of our public education.

It is only natural that people want to enjoy themselves. Everybody does. It's fun to have fun. But where does it lead us? Does all fun and no work still make Johnny a dull boy?

Simultaneous with the increase in recreation, however, has come a serious turn among many of our young people. Millions are seeking a different kind of satisfaction, this time in religion.

Thousands have gone into "Jesus" groups or similar associations. Car stickers announce: "I Found It." Others reply: "I Never Lost It."

Groping as many of them are, there is nevertheless a strong air of genuine sincerity about them. For the most part these youth want whatever is good for them, but they don't know what that is. Sound direction and proper orientation are the needs of the day.

They must know about God: whether he really exists, whether there is a Christ, and whether the gospel can help people today.

Some have seen devout people afflicted with terminal diseases and wondered why they were required to suffer so much. These cases at times almost seemed to challenge their faith.

Anciently Christ taught that his gospel would help people and enrich their lives. The scriptures promised that the heavens would pour out such blessings upon the faithful that they could hardly contain them. And the promise was to all, for the Lord is no respecter of persons.

Our young people ask: If the gospel was that effective anciently, does it or can it or will it work as well today? Can Christ, who is no longer on earth, be a factor in the lives of this modern generation which is so deeply confused?

Probably never before has such a hodgepodge of claims, persuasions, pseudosciences, religious emotions, prophetic-like declarations, misinformation and good and bad entertainment been thrust upon a rising generation. It is done through a wide variety of means, too: television, movies, records, cassettes, youth programs, youth camps, newspapers, magazines, churches, schools, and taverns.

No wonder the young people want clarification! No wonder they demand answers! And they are entitled to them.

Has anyone really wondered why there are so many problems and deviations confronting the young people of today, why there are so many who have turned to drugs, alcohol and sex excitement?

It is simply because most people don't know the purpose in life, don't know why they even exist. They ask why, why? "Are we like bugs and animals or flowers in the garden, here today and gone tomorrow — if there is a tomorrow?"

Many are worried about world conditions, with the possibility of a new war, and ask if they must risk their lives fighting other people's battles.

And then there is something else. Why are there so many dropouts from school? Again, the reason is that students don't know the purpose of their existence, or why going to school can qualify them for greater enjoyment of life.

Many don't want to work, never having learned how. This is why some live on unemployment compensation or other doles. And there is also the involvement in crime. Certain ones would rather steal than work. They know that generally they can get away with it, because a mere fraction of the thieves are caught and only a tiny sampling are ever convicted. Crime pays, they say, and handsomely at that.

The biggest cause of restlessness among our youth is unstable homes. What can we expect of youth who come from broken homes where parental examples have been poor?

It is all evidence of the general lack of knowledge and the total misconception of God, for it is God who gives purpose to life. Nothing else can. And to millions he is an unknown!

Who is Christ? they want to know. Who is God? What are they like? Are they Persons? Or are they merely drifting, shapeless, cloud-like substances filling the universe, as some religious creeds suggest?

Anciently people asked these questions too. The Greeks

of Alexander's day debated them. The early Christian fathers took their turn, as did the Protestant Reformers. And now the radio and TV revivalists are at it.

The basic need of the world today, by which both old and young alike may properly straighten out their lives, is to know God, and to realize that he can and will and does help.

He is not an unknown!

Every one of us can have a personal relationship with God through prayer and righteous living. The companionship of his Spirit is a real thing. It can inspire us, it can whisper warnings in time of need, it can give us a testimony of the importance of prayer in our lives.

God does answer sincere prayer. Hence he can help you solve your problems — right now.

If you have sinned seriously, he will still help you to overcome your weaknesses — right now.

If you feel rejected because of what you may have done, be assured that God will forgive, forget, and help you to rise above the mistakes of life — right now.

If you think no one cares about you, remember that God is your Father. He loves you and can put you back on the road to happiness.

He will not free you from temptation, he will not exempt you from suffering, but he will help you to overcome them. He will show you how to cope with mortal life and succeed. His greatest desire is for us to have the best there is.

But to obtain all of this, we must learn to know him. We must study about him. We must associate ourselves with his Church in an active way, and earn our blessings.

He will not disappoint us if we do our part. We can achieve in school, in love, in marriage, in business, in helping to save other people, and assisting them also to taste the sweet fruits of serving the Lord. Living the gospel is the only sure way to happiness.

Chapter Two

There Is an Answer

W hat can we tell the young person who is sincere and devout in his religion, but who can't figure out answers to some persistent questions?

If there is a God, why does he allow so much wickedness and injustice in the world? Why does he allow war?

If the Bible is true, why are faithful people sometimes made to suffer when wicked ones seem to get off scot-free?

Why do some of our best people have such "bad luck"?

There are very positive answers to these questions.

Of course God lives. The proofs are overwhelming.

Of course the gospel is true. People are abundantly blessed by it.

Of course the Lord can change our lives for the better. He has done it in innumerable cases.

Of course we may have improved living conditions if we serve him.

Of course we can enjoy reasonable prosperity, with health and happiness, through him.

And of course he can be found! He is neither dead nor lost. He is within reach of every human being.

But, some say, we have friends who are very devout, and they have serious diseases, or they have devastating accidents and apparently are not protected from them; or they are afflicted with what most people would simply call bad luck. Why doesn't religion help them?

It is a fact that some are never healed, and some are not protected, and that some, despite their faith and humility, die an early death. However, their faith helps them cope with their problems. It lightens the load.

When we question these things, we must recognize that we simply do not have all of the facts.

We must realize that we are the spirit offspring of God, his literal children. We lived with him in a life which preceded this mortal existence and that life had an effect on this one. We had our free agency there, and could obey or disobey, learn or refuse to learn, advance or drift or even sink into retrogression, just as we pleased, and we brought many of our character traits with us when we entered this life. We had had an eternity of preexistence to form them. Is there any reason to suppose that we would suddenly be free of them, ingrained in our souls as they are?

Indeed, we forgot our preexistence, as God planned, but did that require a change of personality? Note how different individuals are in the same family — any family.

The scriptures tell of the great ones in the spirit world whom God called his leaders. (See Abraham 3:23.) And there was a war in heaven when Satan and his hosts rebelled and fought against God and Christ. These were the two main opposites, but there were many in between.

The faithful ones and the "in-between" ones came to earth as human beings, and are continuing to come. The devil and his imps were thrust down to earth without bodies, to tempt and to try us.

But what was the reasoning in that? It is important to know. We all were to be tested and tried. Some would be tried more than others for reasons known only to God. He knew our acts and intentions and attitudes as we lived in that preexistent life, and he knew what would best persuade us to overcome undesirable tendencies while in mortality. We are all given the opportunity of returning to his presence, but he intended that we should try to perfect ourselves first and come back to him cleansed of our imperfections. That would include personality problems, of course.

What is the purpose of mortal life?

It is that we may develop and become like our Father in heaven. It is natural for mortal children to become like their parents. It is equally natural for us to become like God, our Father, for we have divinity within us, having been born in the spirit as his offspring.

To be like him must include the premise that we will perfect our own lives and become strong by living in his way.

The purpose of the testing on earth is to see whether we really have the mettle of which Gods are made. If we did not bring it with us into mortality, then through suffering and testing here we are given the opportunity of developing it now so that we may take it with us when we depart this life.

God took advantage of Lucifer's war in heaven, and uses Satan to tempt us. Disease takes over at times, perhaps to try our endurance and teach us more patience, or to humble us, or to teach us to say, "Lord, not as I will but as thou wilt."

Life is not just for fun. We realize that Lehi said that man is that he might have joy. But joy and fun are two different things, and our joy as he spoke of it may refer even to an eternity of joy in the world to come, for which we might be better prepared by our obedience here.

We must realize that mortality is part of eternity. Our preexistent life was part of eternity — which is behind us. Our life here is part of eternity, and our life after death and resurrection is the eternity before us. So all phases of our existence are *eternity*. We may compare our being here on earth as a period of schooling to prepare us for the future.

The Lord sees the overall picture. We see it only in the immediate present. Therefore, we do not see it in its fulness. Hence we fail to see in proper perspective the true significance of our experience here.

Although the Lord gives us our free agency so that we can obey or disobey his rules if we like, he nevertheless can and does arrange circumstances which, if we handle them right, will mean eternal advancement for us.

Even Christ himself learned obedience through suffering. Said Paul to the Hebrews: "Though he were a Son, yet learned he obedience by the things which he suffered."

But Paul goes beyond that: "And being made perfect, he became the author of eternal salvation unto all them that obey him." (Hebrews 5:8-9.)

There is much significance there. He suffered in order to learn the added obedience whereby he further perfected himself.

That is symbolic of our own progress toward perfection. We, too, must learn obedience through discipline. We thereby may put our minds and our spirits in tune with him.

We have been told by our leaders that the afflictions many go through during this life will be more than made up to them in the life to come. They will have greater happiness, greater joy, than would otherwise be possible. Discipline and suffering are part of our mortal schooling wherein we become better, purer and bigger souls.

Some seem to go through life scot-free. Some are seldom sick. Some have few or no accidents. Others have many. What is the explanation?

Many difficulties we bring upon ourselves. We cannot blame the Lord for them. Some people have poor health because of the way they eat (or don't eat), their general lifestyle and their personal habits. Others have many accidents because of their wilfulness or thoughtlessness in taking risks. They are spoken of as being "accident-prone."

We are agents unto ourselves. But whereas we may bring some things upon ourselves by our manner of life, admittedly there are other hard experiences which we have no way of accounting for. This reminds us of a case when the Savior healed a man. His disciples asked: "Master, who did sin, this man, or his parents, that he was born blind?" (John 9:2.)

Does this imply that in some instances people did sin in their premortal life and hence suffer in this life in payment for that sin?

The Savior's reply is interesting:

"Neither hath this man sinned, nor his parents: but that the works of God should be made manifest in him." (John 9:3.)

Neither the victim, nor his parents, nor the disciples could explain the affliction of this man, just as we are often unable to explain afflictions in the lives of our friends. But it is clear from this scripture that God has his own purposes.

There are many instances where we bring difficulties upon our own selves. If we expose ourselves to communicable diseases, we may suffer from those illnesses. Many doctors and nurses died of such diseases as smallpox and diphtheria in days past, before we had modern remedies. They gave their lives for others and will be amply rewarded.

But there are other kinds of exposure which are in a different class. For example, those who are immoral often get venereal diseases. When those diseases are not treated medically, they can be passed on to the child of an expectant mother. Who is to blame? Not the child, who is an innocent victim.

But what of that child? Suppose it is born blind or mentally retarded or physically deformed? It suffers, yes. But needlessly? Again we come back to the Savior's example of the blind man.

A spirit was assigned to that child's body. Because of the sin of the parents, the body was deformed. But God is just, and will more than make up to the innocent child here or hereafter for this affliction, and the parents who by sin brought it on the child will be under condemnation.

Or is this a case in which the Old Testament law applies?

"I . . . am a jealous God, visiting the iniquity of the fathers . . . unto the third and fourth generation *of them that hate me*." (Exodus 20:5. Italics added.)

But as we consider this we should keep in mind what Ezekiel said:

"Yet say ye, Why? doth not the son bear the iniquity of the father? When the son hath done that which is lawful and right, and hath kept all my statutes, and hath done them, he shall surely live.

"The soul that sinneth, it shall die. The son shall not bear the iniquity of the father, neither shall the father bear the iniquity of the son: the righteousness of the righteous shall be upon him, and the wickedness of the wicked shall be upon him.

"But if the wicked will turn from all his sins that he hath committed, and keep all my statutes, and do that which is lawful and right he shall surely live, he shall not die.

"All his transgressions that he hath committed, they shall not be mentioned unto him: in his righteousness that he hath done he shall live.

"Have I any pleasure at all that the wicked should die? saith the Lord God: and not that he should return from his ways, and live?

"But when the righteous turneth away from his righteousness, and committeth iniquity, and doeth according to all the abominations that the wicked man doeth, shall he live? All his righteousness that he hath done shall not be mentioned: in his trespass that he hath trespassed, and in his sin that he hath sinned, in them shall he die." (Ezekiel 18:19-24.)

Innocent people are killed by criminals. Why? Who can tell? They may be innocent, and if so God will make up all to them, while punishing the ones responsible for the crime.

Some infants suffer deformities because their mothers smoke or drink, or are unwise in using medication during pregnancy.

We cannot blame God for all these things. Neither can we resent his not healing everyone who is ill, for all must die sometime. When does a person's "time" come? We do not always know what God has in mind.

Some people are appointed unto death. Others are not and may be healed according to the measure of our faith. If our faith is not sufficient to heal them, we should nurse them back to health.

We cannot explain all cases of affliction, and neither can we explain early death or failure of administrations to heal. Even the disciples of Jesus in his day could not cast out an evil spirit in one instance. (See Matthew 17:19-21.)

So we must conclude that in many cases sad experience is to develop faith, the kind of faith which will save our souls.

The Lord's words on this point are interesting:

"And whosoever among you are sick, and have not faith

to be healed, but believe, shall be nourished with all tenderness, with herbs and mild food, and that not by the hand of an enemy.

"And the elders of the church, two or more, shall be called, and shall pray for and lay their hands upon them in my name; and if they die they shall die unto me, and if they live they shall live unto me. . . .

"And it shall come to pass that those that die in me shall not taste of death, for it shall be sweet unto them." (D&C 42:43-46.)

But then he adds: "He that hath faith in me to be healed, *and is not appointed unto death*, shall be healed." (D&C 42:48. Italics added.)

But none of us know what is in God's mind. How can we tell whether a sick person is appointed unto death? It is not revealed to us. Then how can we criticize God? We must have sufficient trust in him to know that he does all things well.

While we are in mortality we are in a purposely arranged situation where hardships come, where natural disasters occur, where diseases are spread, where there are accidents, fires and earthquakes. That is the kind of life we are in, the kind that was intended for our mortal existence to test us and to teach us. It is like being in a drama with stages and curtains and supporting actions.

The big thing to remember is that we do not comprehend all of the Lord's infinite plans, for we are finite. But if we will be faithful to his laws, he will bless us. If we have a hard time in this life, but remain true, he will more than make up for it in the world to come.

And why does this make sense? Because we do not know what we did in our pre-earth life that needed readjustment. We do not know what tendencies or characteristics we had there that need to be corrected here.

We forgot it all when we were born, and intentionally so. But God didn't forget. He knows us in all three phases of our lives — preexistence, earth life, and the life to come — and helps us accordingly, as far as we, with our free agency, allow him to.

Chapter Three

A Great Average

One of our difficulties as we consider the effect of God upon our lives is that we tend to look at individual cases, and overlook the overall situation.

We see a man ninety years old who has smoked all his life. A newspaper reporter asks what made him so healthy. He might say: "I have smoked cigars all my life. I think they have contributed to my longevity."

When we hear that, we know very well that it is false. Tobacco never improves health. Scientific research shows just the opposite.

Then what made the man live so long? Other factors entirely. Maybe he inherited a strong constitution from his parents, maybe he ate well except for his consumption of tobacco, maybe he exercised regularly, maybe many things. But when he said it was the tobacco that gave him long life, we know he was either fooling us or was grossly misled.

We see others who have drunk liquor over the years, and it appears on the surface that it did not hurt them. Or still others who have been immoral seem to suffer no ill effects.

Exceptions really do not prove anything. We must judge the truth and the Lord's blessings to the entire body of the Church by the averages of all our people compared to others.

What kind of a record do we Latter-day Saints have in health?

Note just a few things:

The UCLA School of Public Health at Los Angeles published a report in the *Pasadena Star-News* saying that the incidence of cancer among the Mormons is 50 percent lower than the national average, and in Utah the cancer death rate is the lowest in the United States.

The Statistical Abstract of the United States for the year 1971 (Bureau of the Census) says that Utah is one of the lowest states in the Union with respect to the incidence of a number of other leading diseases.

It ranks forty-sixth in the incidence of heart problems; forty-ninth for influenza and pneumonia; forty-sixth for cerebrovascular diseases; forty-ninth for arteriosclerosis, forty-fifth for cirrhosis of the liver; bronchitis, emphysema and asthma, thirtieth place; major cardiovascular and renal diseases combined, fiftieth place; vascular lesions affecting the nervous system, fiftieth place; hypertensive heart disease, forty-third place; other hypertensive diseases, fiftieth place; complications of pregnancy, forty-sixth place; infant mortality, fiftieth place.

It should be kept in mind that these figures are for the entire state of Utah, where about 30 percent of the population is not Mormon. They are included in the statistics.

These figures point up this important fact: that although there are individual exceptions of which we know, and the reasons for which we do not know, the gospel is effective and operative on a grand scale for the vast majority. That is the "proof of the pudding."

There will always be individual exceptions to almost any situation, but the fact is, that so far as the Latter-day Saints are concerned, the Lord is keeping his promises as made in the scriptures in a spectacular manner.

In individual cases, how did our diseases begin? In many instances we are sheer victims of circumstance, but in some others we bring difficulties upon ourselves, either through our ignorance of health rules, or by our impulsive actions in regard to foods, driving cars, or the company we keep. Let us not blame the Lord for the exceptions.

One of the most regrettable fields in which severe damage comes to individuals is in the matter of birth defects. It is now well accepted by scientists that a large number of babies born with birth defects are injured before birth by their mothers either smoking, drinking liquor, or unwisely using medication.

The child is the victim of someone else's folly, and suffers for it. But again, the Lord does not take away the free agency of the mother. At least in the world to come he will more than make up to the afflicted child all that is lost due to a sad birth.

God is just. If we are handicapped here, we will be compensated either here or hereafter.

In this mortal world we do not pretend to explain or understand every circumstance. Much of what we have here we must accept on faith, knowing full well that God will be fair to all.

Our mortal experience is intended to teach us more about God, inasmuch as it is to help us to become perfect like him. But let us never suppose that God is an unknown, as did the ancient Greeks, for example. He is neither unknown nor unknowable.

Since he desires us to become like him — even commands it — of course he must reveal himself enough so that we can become acquainted with him, and thus emulate his example.

But in the past, man has failed to accept God's overtures as he has sent his prophets to the earth. As a result, darkness and confusion came upon us. Now we need a new light.

Chapter Four

Mars' Hill – Today

When the apostle Paul visited Athens, he found the city given over to idolatry, but he saw one altar that gave him hope. It was marked: "To the Unknown God." It provided him with an opportunity to declare the truth about the Creator to those intelligent Greeks.

The Almighty is still an unknown to nearly all peoples of the earth today. But as was the case in Paul's day, a glimmer of light and hope now appears.

Both advanced science and revealed religion declare that God lives and is a reality.

More and more, men of learning take the attitude of Dr. Arthur H. Compton, Nobel prize winner, who said over forty years ago: "Few scientific men today defend the atheistic attitude. The more we learn about the world in which we live, the less the probability that it is a product of chance. Never yet has there been adequate refutation of the argument that design in the universe presumes an intelligence. Evidence points to the existence of a Beginner, a Creator of the Universe. A physicist's studies lead him to believe this Creator to be an intelligent Being." (*This Week* magazine, *Los Angeles Times*, Easter issue, 1936.)

And from one of the world's leading scientists of today we have:

"It is natural for me to worship the Supreme Intelligence of the universe, and I am convinced that, wise as men are and in spite of the wonderful things they have done, the Creator of this universe goes so far beyond anything that men understand that it is ridiculous to talk of the two in the same terms. . . .

"Since all truth has a single source, the apparent conflicts [between science and religion] that often trouble us reflect only our incomplete understanding.

"I believe that every brilliant conquest made by man is but a manifestation of the divine spark which sets him apart from the rest of creation.

"Man is in the image of God, destined to go on learning and perfecting himself throughout eternity. To accept the idea that the human personality ends with death is to accept life as a futile, meaningless gesture." (Henry Eyring, *The Faith of a Scientist* [Salt Lake City: Bookcraft, 1967], pp. 107, 184.)

It was Dr. Oscar Leo Brauer, physicist at San Jose State College, who said: "Science can establish that a creative act at some time must have taken place, implying the existence of a Divine Intelligence and a Divine Power. Science can also establish that none *but* a Divine Intelligence could have been the Author of the tremendous, involved and intricate system of laws in the universe." (Oscar Leo Brauer, "The Most Vital Question Confronting Us," *The Evidence of God in an Expanding Universe*, John Clover Monsma, ed. (New York: G. P. Putnam's Sons, 1958); p. 84. Italics added.)

When Sir Francis Younghusband wrote for quotation in Mason's *The Great Design*, he said: "Intelligence and will must have existed and been operative long before the earth was [formed]." (Frances Mason, editor, *The Great Design* [New York: The Macmillan Company, 1934], p. 252.)

Einstein said: "The harmony of natural law . . . reveals an intelligence of such superiority that, compared with it, all the systematic thinking and acting of human beings is an utterly insignificant reflection." (Albert Einstein, *The World As I See It* [New York: The Philosophical Library, 1949], p. 29.)

He also added: "The most incomprehensible thing about the world is that it is comprehensible. . . . To this [sphere of religion] there also belongs the faith in the possibility that the regulations valid for the world of existence are rational, that is comprehensible."

After explaining that a scientist could not do his work without profound faith, he continued: "The situation may be expressed by an image: science without religion is lame, religion without science is blind." (Paul Arthur Schlipp, editor, *Albert Einstein, Philosopher-Scientist* [New York: Tudor Publishing Company, 1957], pp. 284, 285.)

So much for the wisdom of men. The wisdom of God gives us unerring and direct answers. God lives. He has appeared to mortals. God lives. He has spoken directly to them, both ancient and modern. God lives and has raised up prophets who are his earthly spokesmen. God lives and has given us the sacred record and vital testimony of scripture. God lives!

He is not unknowable. Rather, he opens the door to us, and invites us to become acquainted with him, actually reminding us that without knowing him there is no salvation. No one can be saved in ignorance. The glory of God is knowledge and intelligence. The glory of man — if he will accept it — is a knowledge of God and the intelligence to understand how to use it.

Did not Jesus invite us to *know* him and to follow him? "Learn of me," he said, "and ye shall find rest unto your souls." (Matthew 11:29.) Then can we find rest to our souls unless we do come to know him? He is not unknowable!

He also said, "Come unto me, all ye that labour and are heavy laden, and I will give you rest." (Matthew 11:28.)

If he were unknowable, incomprehensible and .unapproachable, would he have extended such an invitation?

He also urged us to search the scriptures as a means of knowing and understanding him, "for they are they which testify of me." (John 5:39.)

And beyond all that, he commands us to become *like* him, even *perfect* as our Father in heaven. (See Matthew 5:48.) And this would be impossible with either the unknowable or the unknown.

Certainly by coming to know him we can open the door to worship him with some measure of intelligence. Worship of an unknown is but a blind and useless exercise which can accomplish nothing and which hardly seems to make sense in any case.

When Paul came to Athens and saw the flagrant idolatry on Mars' Hill, he discovered that those intelligent Greeks sensed that there was more to divine worship than bowing before handmade images. They, of course, had numerous gods in their mythology — Zeus, Apollo, Neptune, Hades, and the rest. But obviously they had a feeling that beyond all of those conjured-up divinities was some greater Power whom they could not identify but whom they called the "Unknown God."

Paul deplored their idolatry and said: "Ye men of Athens, I perceive that in all things ye are too superstitious.

"For as I passed by, and beheld your devotions, I found an altar with this inscription, TO THE UNKNOWN GOD. Whom therefore ye ignorantly worship, him declare I unto you.

"God that made the world and all things therein, seeing that he is Lord of heaven and earth, dwelleth not in temples made with hands;

"Neither is worshipped with men's hands, as though he needed any thing, seeing he giveth to all life, and breath, and all things;

"And hath made of one blood all nations of men for to dwell on all the face of the earth, and hath determined the times before appointed, and the bounds of their habitation." (Acts 17:22-26.)

As he spoke to them of this true God, he referred to the teachings of their own poets, who said, "For we are also his offspring."

Making this point, he again launched out against idolatry, and said: "Forasmuch then as we are the offspring of God, we ought not to think that the Godhead is like unto gold, or silver, or stone, graven by art and man's device." (Acts 17:28-29.)

He branded that as ignorance and said that now God commands all men to repent. (See Acts 17:30.)

Paul spoke to them in terms which they understood, and did not hesitate to refer to their poetic doctrine that man is the child of God. Instead, he seized upon it, for the doctrine was true.

The Greeks undoubtedly quoted their poets correctly, but who among them could explain the mystery of their words?

Mortal man — could he really be the child of God? The Almighty Creator — was he actually the progenitor of human beings?

They had been told in their mythology that the pagan gods came down and mingled with mortals, even having children by them. Is that what the poets meant?

Also, according to their myths, the Greek divinities consorted with human beings, at which time there was anything but a holy influence about them, for they liked fun, and evil fun at that. They shunned responsibility for their deeds after being involved in mischief on the earth, and would escape like children in a prank, seeking the refuge of heaven lest some fearful retribution overtake them.

Did the poets have gods of this kind in mind when they wrote the words which Paul quoted?

Chapter Five

What Paul Meant

When the Greek poets wrote that man is the offspring of God, and Paul confirmed it, what did they mean? What did Paul mean?

This apostle to the gentiles was teaching the Greeks the same doctrine which he taught both the Romans and the Hebrews. He made it clear in his subsequent teachings that man is a dual being, consisting of both body and spirit; that the spirit is the real person or individual, the body being a physical house in which the spirit lives.

It is that spirit which is the offspring of God. It is eternal, and because it is a child of God, it has divinity within it and can never die. Paul wrote these important words to the Hebrews:

"Furthermore we have had fathers of our flesh which corrected us, and we gave them reverence: shall we not much rather be in subjection unto the Father of spirits, and live?" (Hebrews 12:9.)

Obviously there was no doubt in Paul's mind. He understood the scriptures. He had received revelations from God, including a vision of the Savior. He knew that Jesus was the Son of God. He knew, too, that the Savior also taught that God is our Father. God is truly the Father of our spirits.

To the Romans Paul gave further light, as he wrote:

"The Spirit itself beareth witness with our spirit, that we are the children of God:

"And if children, then heirs; heirs of God, and joint-heirs with Christ; if so be that we suffer with him, that we may be also glorified together." (Romans 8:16-17.)

There is a great truth here, often overlooked. As we have already seen, we are spirits residing in human bodies and as such we are the spirit children of God. Physical bodies are mortal dwellings for the spirits during their sojourn here.

Being the children of God, we can, if we do right, become like our Father in Heaven — heirs of God, to use Paul's expression. We can become joint heirs with Christ, says Paul.

Who is Jesus? He is our Savior, our Redeemer and our Lord. He is one of the Godhead. (See Colossians 2:9; Romans 1:20; Acts 17:29.) He is divine! May we sometime in the eternities become like him? It was Jesus who taught us that we are destined to become perfect even as God is perfect, if we keep his commandments.

As Paul speaks of the Godhead, what does he mean? Modern churches mention the Trinity, but confuse it with their doctrine of "not three gods but one god, not three incomprehensibles but one. . . ."

The Godhead consists of the Father, Son and Holy Ghost, working together as three separate Beings in one vast undertaking to save mankind, each working in his own sphere. Jesus was the Savior. He died on the cross for our sins, and brought about the Resurrection whereby all may come forth from the grave.

The Holy Ghost is the Comforter, whom Jesus said he would send after his departure from the earth. (See John 14:15-31.)

The Father is that mighty Deity to whom Jesus gave such reverence, and who is above all things, and our Heavenly Progenitor.

But they are separate Personages, as the Prophet Joseph Smith explained:

"The Father has a body of flesh and bones as tangible as man's; the Son also; but the Holy Ghost has not a body of flesh and bones, but is a personage of Spirit. Were it not so, the Holy Ghost could not dwell in us." (D&C 130:22.)

Such is the Godhead. And we mortals are invited to become perfect, even as they are. This, of course, we must do by living according to all the laws of God.

In just a few words Jesus explained the whole existence of man and portrayed the divine destiny that lies before us. Said he:

"Be ye therefore perfect, even as your Father which is in heaven is perfect." (Matthew 5:48.)

Then there can be no doubt. Since we are his children and his heirs — heirs to the riches of eternity, heirs to the same kind of blessings and the glorious destiny personified in the Christ — we can truly become like him. That is the whole point and purpose of our existence.

To contemplate this estate carries us beyond the remotest flight of our imagination. God is the Almighty. Yet in eternity man may become like him!

But as we consider these things, let us remember always that God is infinite, far beyond the human ability to measure, and that we are mere finite, weak, mortal beings, almost like the dust before him.

He is the Creator of all things. We are but struggling earthlings, but he has given us an infinite potential, since we have a spark of divinity within us. We have been born of God as his spirit children.

On Mars' Hill Paul taught the Greeks that the Lord was not made by human hands, out of gold, or silver, or stone, graven by art and man's device.

He is the great Giver of all. It is out of his infinite abundance that we receive life and breath and the food that grows for our sustenance. "In him we live and move and have our being," this courageous apostle taught.

Our actual existence, then, is a gift of God, both our life here in mortality and our eternal life which is yet to come. In the eternities we may exercise our right of heirship as we gradually develop those traits of character, those abilities and that knowledge which will help us to become like him.

What a marvelous destiny lies before us! How great is Almighty God! And how merciful!

Let us not suppose, however, that all of God's blessings are for the eternities. In mortality we may enjoy peace, health, security and happiness as present-day rewards for obedience. In this life he is our Comfort, our Refuge and our great Helper.

Jesus spoke often of God as our Father. He did so even in prayer and gave us a model to follow as he opened the Lord's prayer with, "Our Father which art in heaven, Hallowed be thy name."

And then, in that same Sermon on the Mount, he added: "If ye forgive men their trespasses, your heavenly Father will also forgive you."

Many of his other teachings include reference to God as our Father. For example:

"Love your enemies. . . . that ye may be the children of your Father which is in heaven." (Matthew 5:44-45.)

"Be not ye therefore like unto them [the heathens]: for your Father knoweth what things ye have need of." (Matthew 6:8.)

"Thy Father which seeth in secret shall reward thee openly." (Matthew 6:6.)

"Your heavenly Father knoweth that ye have need of all these things." (Matthew 6:32.)

And especially do we remember this important statement made by the Lord after his resurrection:

"I ascend unto my Father, and your Father; and to my God, and your God." (John 20:17.)

So God is our Father, and we are made in his image. Jesus, his beloved and divine Son, came to be like his Father, and we have the potential of sometime becoming like Jesus. What a concept! What a staggering thought!

Our Heavenly Father is a genuine Person, and a loving

Parent, a Model after whom we should plan our lives, even as Jesus, who did nothing but what he saw his Father do. (See John 5:19.)

Then who and what is God? Not only is he our Father, he is the great Pattern of the ultimate in man's possible development. And what is man? He is divinity in embryo.

Chapter Six

The Divine Person

No one reading either history or the scriptures can reasonably doubt that Jesus Christ was and is a Person. He once had a mortal, physical body, but was subsequently resurrected, still with a physical body of flesh and bones. (See John 20:20; Luke 24:39.)

He was a great reality! He was born as the Babe in Bethlehem. He was cradled in a manager. He was visited by the shepherds and the wise men. He was such a reality that the wicked King Herod, in a fit of jealousy, tried to kill him. He did destroy many other little babies, hoping Jesus would be one of them. He stopped at nothing in his effort to protect his throne. Since Jesus was hailed as the king of the Jews, Herod could not tolerate him.

Jesus was taken into Egypt for safety, and later returned to Nazareth.

As an infant, he was taken to the temple in Jerusalem where a sacrifice of two young pigeons was made. And there devout Simeon had it revealed to him that Jesus — this little child — was the Christ. He took the little one in his arms and blessed him.

And Anna, a prophetess laboring in the temple, "spake of him to all them that looked for redemption in Jerusalem."

The scripture adds: "And when they had performed all things according to the law of the Lord, they returned into Galilee to their own city of Nazareth.

"And the child grew and waxed strong in the spirit, filled with wisdom, and the grace of God was upon him." (Luke 2:38-40.)

He was raised in the environs of a carpenter shop. At twelve years of age he was taken to Jerusalem for the Passover and there talked with the priests in the temple.

He was baptized of John in Jordan, literally and physically. He called disciples to follow him and they responded, even leaving house and home and business to do so.

He hungered at times, and knew fatigue. He slept as other people did, and he wept on occasion. He often seemed friendless, and was severely persecuted, ultimately being arrested and whipped before crucifixion. It was a real physical scourging, and a literal and cruel physical crucifixion.

He looked so much like other men that when his enemies finally prepared to crucify him, they could not identify him, so they needed a Judas to point him out so that they would not kill the wrong man. They actually could not distinguish Jesus from his disciples, he was so much like them in appearance.

And yet, Jesus resembled his Father in heaven. So close was this resemblance that he himself said, "He that hath seen me hath seen the Father." (John 14:9.) Is not God a Person?

In the Creation, God made man in his own image and likeness. Because various creeds have confused the meaning of those words, a sure definition is required for proper understanding.

The Bible provides that definition in reference to the birth of Seth, the son of Adam. The scripture reads:

"This is the book of the generations of Adam. In the day that God created man, in the likeness of God made he him;

"Male and female created he them; and blessed them, and called their name Adam, in the day when they were created.

"And Adam lived an hundred and thirty years, and begat a son in his own likeness, after his image; and called his name Seth:

"And the days of Adam after he had begotten Seth were eight hundred years: and he begat sons and daughters." (Genesis 5:1-4.)

As Seth looked like his father Adam, being in his image and likeness, so Adam looked like God, being in his image and likeness, says this passage. The same words are used in both instances in the same few verses to express identical thoughts. It is a clear definition of terms.

Now let us look at it this way:

Since Adam was in the image and likeness of God, and Seth was in the image and likeness of Adam, was not Seth also in the image and likeness of God? Of course! And so was Enos, the son of Seth, and so was Cainan, the son of Enos, and so was Mahalaleel, the son of Cainan, and so are we, who live today, for we are the descendants of Adam, every one of us.

We are all of one race, the race of God. Man can only reproduce man, and man was always man. All life brings forth only after its own kind, even human life. Has any human ever brought forth any kind of life but human?

Since we are of the race of God, it is possible, reasonable, and factual that we may become perfect as he is. By our birth in his race, we have this great potential inherently within us. That is why we can become heirs of God and joint heirs with Christ.

Could we become *like* God if we were in different form and shape *from* God? Could a rose be other than a rose? Could man be other than man? Can a child of God be other than his offspring? Can any offspring be of a different species from the parent?

In the Creation, all life was commanded to reproduce itself after its own kind, and only so. Through all the generations since the Creation the various life species have held true. Wheat is always wheat, corn is always corn, birds are always birds and man is always man.

Man was born as the offspring of God, who obeyed his own law of generation as set forth in Genesis. Hence, as his children, we are in his image and likeness just as surely as were Adam and Seth and Enos.

When Jesus ascended to heaven he sat down on the right hand of God. (See Hebrews 1:1-3.)

Moses walked and talked with God (see Exodus 33:9-23; Numbers 12:7-8), as did Noah and Enoch (see Genesis 6:9; 5:18-24; Hebrews 11:7; Jude 14, 15). Are not such occurrences part of our definition of the form and shape and faculties of God?

As the Savior was ascending to heaven, two angels stood near the disciples and told them that the Lord would come again "in like manner as ye have seen him go into heaven." (Acts 1:11.) Then would he not retain his recognizable form and shape and thus appear in the Second Coming?

When Joseph Smith and Sidney Rigdon received the vision described in Doctrine and Covenants 76, they saw both the Father and the Son, whose form and shape had not been changed through the centuries. They were fully identifiable.

Joseph Smith's declaration in Doctrine and Covenants 130 clearly shows all three of the Godhead to be Persons, separate and individual.

How could we become like them otherwise? How could we become heirs of God except he were a Person, inasmuch as we are persons?

No universal, shapeless essence, unknown and inexplainable, could bequeath anything to us as heirs, but a divine Person can, and does and will!

Chapter Seven

Idols and Christianity

The Christians were completely surrounded by idol worshippers, even as ancient Israel had been. It was a constant battle with them to avoid that evil influence.

The residence of a great many Greeks in Palestine made the threat of idolatry a very real one. Since the conquest by Alexander the Great, thousands of Greeks had been moved by their government into the conquered territories, including Palestine, setting up colonies of Greek citizens who brought their own customs, culture and religion with them.

It had been Alexander's plan, and that of his successors, to prevent any uprising in the conquered territories by placing Greek soldiers, businessmen and educators in these colonies, together with their families, as permanent settlers. In this way Greek communities were established in the conquered countries, including the Holy Land.

It is a mistake to suppose that the Jews had Palestine all to themselves during the days of Christ, or for centuries before and after.

Under both Greek and Roman rule, Greek culture was advocated and preserved in those conquered lands. Greek games were played there, amphitheaters were built, and a serious effort was made to "hellenize" all of the conquered populations.

King Herod the Great was one of the leaders in this undertaking, and carried it a long way in Palestine.

Arnold Toynbee, editor of the great book *The Crucible of Christianity*, says:

"Herod took the initiative . . . to open the doors to foreign cultural influences. . . . He pursued this policy in his grandiose Hellenistic way by spending fabulous sums of money on a number of Greek cities [in the Holy Land].

"He equipped them munificently with huge public buildings: markets, theatres, aqueducts, promenades, and other public works of social consequence.

"He introduced Greek artists and men of letters into his dominions and founded musical festivals and public games, to which many foreign non-Jewish guests were invited, even in Jerusalem. . . .

"In a word, Herod tried, if only partially, to remove the fence with which, under the guidance of the Pharisees, the Jewish religion had surrounded the Jewish people. He tried to integrate the Jews in the Hellenistic-Roman [way of life]. . . . [He tried to integrate] the Jewish people in the gentile world." (Arnold Toynbee, ed., *The Crucible of Christianity* [New York: World Publishing Co., 1969], pp. 72-73.)

To bring Greek culture, games and education into Palestine meant also the introduction of their pagan religions. This the Christians had to face constantly.

As an evidence of the danger which the ancient Twelve Apostles saw in this formidable enemy to truth, it is recalled that the brethren sent Paul, Barnabas and Silas to Antioch (a gentile city) with a special message opposing idolatry. They emphasized that all there who had joined the Church were to "abstain from pollutions of idols, and from fornication, and from things strangled, and from blood." (Acts 15:20.)

Idolatry, in a very real sense, was a pollution to those early Christians. As they brought idol-worshipping gentiles into the Church, it became an issue with each convert, just as did circumcision.

Idolatry was bad enough in that it was a repudiation of the true God in favor of handmade images, but with some ancient peoples it was a sex perversion as well. The goddesses were sex symbols of fertility and their worship required the patronage of temple prostitutes, male and female. It was the sex attraction which made idolatry as popular as it was.

When the Greek people in Jerusalem were converted to the Church and began to participate in its activities, they became a highly vocal group to be sure. They were intellectually strong. They were very independent, and they insisted on their rights. This is evidenced by the following scripture:

"And in those days, when the number of the disciples was multiplied, there arose a murmuring of the Grecians against the Hebrews, because their widows were neglected in the daily ministration.

"Then the twelve called the multitude of the disciples unto them, and said, It is not reason that we should leave the word of God, and serve tables.

"Wherefore, brethren, look ye out among you seven men of honest report, full of the Holy Ghost and wisdom, whom we may appoint over this business.

"But we will give ourselves continually to prayer, and to the ministry of the word.

"And the saying pleased the whole multitude: and they chose Stephen, a man full of faith and of the Holy Ghost, and Philip, and Prochorus, and Nicanor, and Timon, and Parmenas, and Nicolas a proselyte of Antioch:

"Whom they set before the apostles: and when they had prayed, they laid their hands on them.

"And the word of God increased; and the number of the disciples multiplied in Jerusalem greatly; and a great company of the priests were obedient to the faith." (Acts 6:1-7.)

Paul's reference to the Greeks in many places in his writings further reflects the influence of that race in early Christianity. For example:

"For I am not ashamed of the gospel of Christ: for it is the power of God unto salvation to every one that believeth; to the Jew first, and also to the Greek." (Romans 1:16.)

To make certain that both Jews and Greeks were given equal treatment in the Church, Paul taught:

"For there is no difference between the Jew and the Greek: for the same Lord over all is rich unto all that call upon him." (Romans 10:12.)

Greek brethren were placed in the ministry also. For example, Timothy, known also as Timotheus, was the son of a Greek father and a Jewish mother. He lived at Lystra. (See Acts 16:1.) It is believed that Timothy was converted on Paul's first journey to that area.

Titus lived on the island of Crete, in the Greek Archipelago, and became a bishop there. He was no doubt of that nationality, although there is no specific record on this point.

Other gentiles also were brought into prominence in the Church, as is evidenced from Paul's epistles in which he mentions Artemas, Tychicus, and Zenos in the letter to Titus; Priscilla, Aquila, Onesiphorus, Trophimus, Limus, Claudia, Pudens, and Eubulus, all in the second epistle to Timothy.

The prominence of the Greeks and the fact that the Greek culture was *the* culture of the day, was responsible for the New Testament appearing in the Greek language at that early time.

We should not be confused by the presence of Greek culture under Roman rule in Palestine and elsewhere. The Romans liked Greek culture better than their own, and fostered it. Hence Roman rule and Greek culture existed jointly in the Holy Land as well as in other conquered countries.

When the Romans sacked Jerusalem in A.D. 70 they drove away the devout Jews who were not killed in the war, whether they were Christians or followers of the law of Moses. Then Greek influence became greater than ever in Jerusalem. In the time of Hadrian, Roman emperor from A.D. 117 to 138, Jerusalem was known as a Greek city.

Of course idolatry had plagued ancient Israel in Old Testament times. It will be remembered that Elijah battled the

450 priests of Baal when the Israelites defiled the land by putting up shrines to the heathen gods.

The fiasco of Solomon, yielding to his heathen wives and setting up idols for them in his land, brought about his own destruction and hastened the division of the Twelve Tribes.

The Lord most sternly commanded the people to avoid all other gods and to serve him alone. In the Ten Commandments he had said:

"Thou shalt have no other gods before me. Thou shalt not make unto thee any graven image, or any likeness of anything that is in the heaven above, or that is in the earth beneath, or that is in the water under the earth: Thou shalt not bow down thyself to them, nor serve them." (Exodus 20:4.)

The Israelites had fought off idolatry in Egypt and were brought into the Promised Land only to find that it, too, was filled with pagan people. The Lord warned them and forewarned them against the "pollution of idols."

But with it all, since so many Greeks were transplanted into Palestine, bringing their idols with them, the situation was greatly complicated.

Although there are no census figures to support the claim, some historians feel that there were at least a fourth as many Greeks or their descendants in Palestine in Christ's day as there were Jews. Of course, there were also Romans and other nationals. Following the Babylonian captivity, when most Jews were taken out of Palestine, the gentile population naturally enough prevailed and gained a firm foothold.

There was definitely a strong mix of Greek and Jew in the Holy Land and this eventually was a great factor in the downfall of the true Christian religion.

One of the worst of the idolatrous movements in Old Testament times came in the period of Jeremiah, six hundred years before Christ. There developed among the Israelites the foreign doctrine of the queen of heaven or the supreme mother of heaven, which sprang up again in Christianity during the Dark Ages.

In rebuking this false doctrine, the prophet Jeremiah forcefully said:

"Seest thou not what they do in the cities of Judah and in the streets of Jerusalem?

"The children gather wood, and the fathers kindle the fire, and the women knead their dough, to make cakes to the queen of heaven, and to pour out drink offerings unto other gods, that they may provoke me to anger.

"Do they provoke me to anger? saith the Lord: do they not provoke themselves to the confusion of their own faces?

"Therefore thus saith the Lord God; Behold, mine anger and my fury shall be poured out upon this place, upon man, and upon beast, and upon the trees of the field, and upon the fruit of the ground; and it shall burn, and shall not be quenched.

"Thus saith the Lord of hosts, the God of Israel; Put your burnt offerings unto your sacrifices, and eat flesh.

"For I spake not unto your fathers, nor commanded them in the day that I brought them out of the land of Egypt, concerning burnt offerings or sacrifices:

"But this thing commanded I them, saying, Obey my voice, and I will be your God, and ye shall be my people: and walk ye in all the ways that I have commanded you, that it may be well unto you.

"But they hearkened not, nor inclined their ear, but walked in the counsels and in the imagination of their evil heart, and went backward, and not forward.

"Since the day that your fathers came forth out of the land of Egypt unto this day I have even sent unto you all my servants the prophets, daily rising up early and sending them:

"Yet they hearkened not unto me, nor inclined their ear, but hardened their neck: they did worse than their fathers." (Jeremiah 7:17-26.)

And then the courageous Jeremiah was commanded of the Lord in this language:

"Therefore thou shalt speak all these words unto them; but they will not hearken to thee: thou shalt also call unto them; but they will not answer thee.

"But thou shalt say unto them, This is a nation that

obeyeth not the voice of the Lord their God, nor receiveth correction: truth is perished, and is cut off from their mouth.

"Cut off thine hair, O Jerusalem, and cast it away, and take up a lamentation on high places; for the Lord hath rejected and forsaken the generation of his wrath.

"For the children of Judah have done evil in my sight, saith the Lord: they have set their abominations in the house which is called by my name, to pollute it.

"And they have built the high places of Tophet, which is in the valley of the son of Hinnom, to burn their sons and their daughters in the fire; which I commanded them not, neither came it into my heart." (Jeremiah 7:27-31.)

In the forty-fourth chapter of Jeremiah, the prophet repeated his warnings against idolatry and worship of the queen of heaven. The women of the day seem to have been the worst offenders. The scripture reads:

"Then all the men which knew that their wives had burned incense unto other gods, and all women that stood by, a great multitude, even all the people that dwelt in the land of Egypt, in Pathros, answered Jeremiah, saying,

"As for the word that thou hast spoken unto us in the name of the Lord, we will not hearken unto thee.

"But we will certainly do whatsoever thing goeth forth out of our own mouth, to burn incense unto the queen of heaven, and to pour out drink offerings unto her, as we have done, we, and our fathers, our kings, and our princes, in the cities of Judah, and in the streets of Jerusalem: for then had we plenty of victuals, and were well, and saw no evil.

"But since we left off to burn incense to the queen of heaven, and to pour out drink offerings unto her, we have wanted all things, and have been consumed by the sword and by the famine.

"And when we burned incense to the queen of heaven, and poured out drink offerings unto her, did we make her cakes to worship her, and pour out drink offerings unto her, without our men?" (Jeremiah 44:15-19.)

The Babylonian captivity was still another case in which the Jews wrestled with the problem of idolatry. The story of the three Hebrew children and King Nebuchadnezzar is typical. The Hebrews resisted the pressure of the king, it will be remembered; at least this was true of the three who were thrown into the fire. (See Daniel 3.) No one knows how many others may have bowed to the idol rather than risk their own lives.

Idolatry — having other gods — has been the bane of the work of the Lord from earliest times. It is still with us in a slightly different form.

Chapter Eight

Greek Philosophers

The presence of so many Greeks in Palestine meant also the presence of Greeks within the membership of the Church, for many joined. This was inevitable.

Paul in his day strongly warned against the encroachment of philosophy into the Church. He said to the Colossians:

"Beware lest any man spoil you through philosophy and vain deceit, after the tradition of men, after the rudiments of the world, and not after Christ." (Colossians 2:8.)

When Greeks came into the Church they brought with them their education and their influence. Philosophy was an all-important element in Greek life. So was debate. There were many schools of philosophy among them and no one ever lacked opportunity to argue some issue.

Augustine in *The City of God* mentions this at length, and after saying that there were 288 different schools of Greek philosophical thought in his day, he writes that each was "the inventor of his own dogma and opinion" and adds, there were "very many of them, whose love of truth severed them from their teachers ... that they might strive for what they thought was the truth, whether it was so or not."

Augustine then continues: "Among the multitude of philosophers, who in their work have left . . . monuments of their dogmas, no one will easily find any who agree in all their opinions." (Saint Augustine, *The City of God* [New York: Random House, 1950], p. 649.)

He then mentions the Stoics, the Epicureans, the Athenians, and the followers of Jupiter and says that much of their discussion had to do with religion. The Greeks were interested in it and by the hour, the month and the year they disputed over the nature of God.

Four hundred years before Christ, Plato was doing this, and four hundred years after Christ, Augustine was still doing it.

Augustine then describes the philosophers of his day, who differed little from those of two hundred years earlier, and says:

"Yet did not each gather disciples to follow his own sect? Indeed, in the conspicuous and well-known porch, in gymnasia, in gardens, in places public and private, they openly strove in bands each for his own opinion, some asserting there was one world, others innumerable worlds; some that this world had a beginning, others that it had not; some that it would perish, others that it would exist always; some that it was governed by the divine mind, others by chance and accident; some that souls are immortal, others that they are mortal, and of those who asserted their immortality, some said they transmigrated through beasts, others that it was by no means so, while of those who asserted their mortality, some said they [the souls] perished immediately after the body, others that they survived either a little while or a longer time, but not always."

He gives further description in these words:

"Now what people, senate, power, or public dignity of the impious city has ever taken care to judge between all these and other well-nigh innumerable dissensions of the philosophers, approving and accepting some, and disapproving and rejecting others? . . .

"Even if some true things were said, . . . yet falsehoods were uttered with the same licence; so that such a city has not amiss received the title of the mystic Babylon. For Babylon means confusion. . . . Nor does it matter to the devil, its king, how they wrangle among themselves in contradictory errors, since all alike deservedly belong to him on account of their great and varied impiety." (Saint Augustine, *The City of God,* pp. 649-650.)

Philosophers such as these infiltrated the Church, and certainly by this time there was much room for debate there. The question of the nature of God, for example, had never been settled by the Greeks, and now Christianity opened up an entirely new forum.

It will be remembered that all through the first several centuries of Christianity the Church was strictly an Eastern one, and so was the wave of philosophy that engulfed it. One of the major centers of the philosophers was Alexandria in Egypt. Constantinople became another after its construction by Constantine the Great, who moved the center of government and of culture to his new city. There also he set up what he considered to be the headquarters of the Christian Church.

And why not? He had a sense of ownership concerning it. He had endowed it financially. He had begun appointing the leading clergy (although he was not so much as a member of the Church at that time), and gave it generous direction.

He was not a man of learning, but he admired scholars, and the philosophers were the scholars.

Religiously speaking, at this time Rome was of little or no importance to the Christians. Constantinople had become the center of the government and nearly everything else, and to it many of the leaders in all lines of thought were drawn.

And who were the leaders of the Christian Church in those days? Not the westerners, and not Rome, for Rome was west. Actually, Rome did little to built up its case in church leadership until nearly the time of Gregory, about A.D. 600, when the civil government was in collapse.

Gregory, a strong, aspiring and ambitious man, assumed to lead both church and state. He ascended to power in the midst of political upheaval in Italy after the country was thrown into confusion by the Lombards — who had invaded that land twenty years before the rise of Gregory.

In the early centuries, since the Church was definitely Eastern, its scholarly leaders were largely related to the schools in Alexandria, Constantinople and Antioch. Most of the members of the Church and most of its leaders lived in Asia Minor in what is now Turkey, and also in North Africa.

In all the religious confusion of those days, the true God was still very much "unknown." The scholars, however, saw an opportunity for an easy transition from the Greek mythological divinities to the Godhead of the Christians, and were perfectly willing to exchange religious ideas with the Christians, including the use of their images.

For example, Greek artists took statues of Apollo and the Mithraic monuments and used them with slight modifications for Christian personalities and biblical scenes. It was not long before symbolism in art and allegory in literature became important Christian characteristics, the mysteries of the faith being told in parable or veiled in sign and symbol. Christianity retained much of the old classical culture even into the Middle Ages.

As the Greek teachers began to accept Christian ideals, they found that they could get along without Zeus and Neptune, for they now had found a God in Christ. They sought to crystallize their new ideas of Deity by using images which now suddenly ceased to be idols, and representing them simply as a means of visualizing the Christian God. This approach appeased both gentiles and Christians without really denying the pagan gods. Hence, the Greeks, the Romans and the Egyptians found new expression in this form of Christianity. But they still were without the "unknown" God.

Chapter Nine

The Council of Nicaea

When Constantine took over the Christian Church, he found that it was more splintered even than his Roman empire had been. To make the Church helpful to him it would have to be fused into a unified force. So he called the Nicene Council to settle the main point of dissension — the nature of God.

As further evidence that the Church was strictly an Eastern one, it is noted that Nicaea (see the map) was chosen for this gathering of bishops because of its more central location in the East. It was in what today is Turkey. Rome was not so much as considered. Few representatives came from the West, and none at all from Rome, which had little if anything to offer Christianity in that day but discord.

The work of the council centered in a debate over the nature of God. That question had to be settled if any degree of unity were to come to the Church.

Constantine chose two protagonists, both of them Greek philosophers. They were Arius and Athanasius. Arius denied the prevailing doctrine that Jesus and our Heavenly Father are of one and the same substance.

Athanasius, bishop of Alexandria, was spoken of by early Christians as the father of orthodoxy. He advocated the

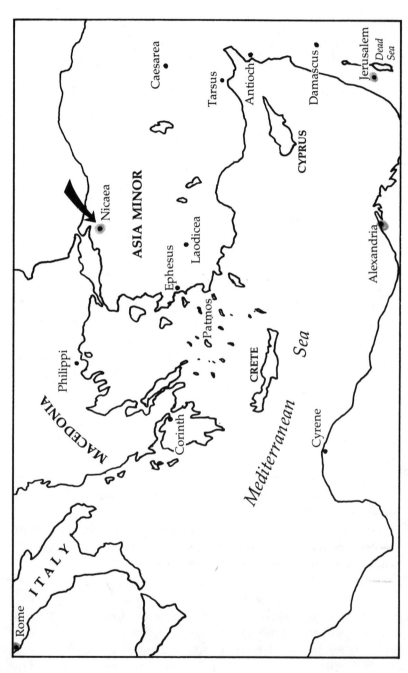

ASIA MINOR AT THE TIME OF THE NICAEAN COUNCIL IN THE FOURTH CENTURY

three-in-one concept of Deity. His doctrine prevailed and is still accepted by many modern denominations.

Definitions of the Holy Ghost virtually abolished Him.

What chance did the truth have in this situation? Where was revelation? Where were the pure doctrines of Christ, now drowned in a relentless stream of philosophy? Where was divine authority?

The Nicene Creed was devised strictly and unquestionably through Greek thought and Greek debate.

The two opponents were Greek. Their training was Greek. Their method of debate was unadulterated Athenian. And the creed that came out of the entire disaster was a direct reflection of the efforts made to brew an impossible potion by mixing idolatry with the gospel.

Dr. A. E. Burn speaking of Arius in *The Council of Nicaea* says, among other things:

"Arianism then was almost as much a philosophy as a religion. It assumed the usual philosophical postulates, worked by the usual philosophical methods, and scarcely referred to Scripture except in quest of isolated texts to confirm conclusions reached without its help."

Of Athanasius he says:

"By birth and education Athanasius was a Greek, a Greek in noble thoughts and philosophic insight, an orator and a statesman." He was of the Antioch school of philosophy, another center of Greek thought. (A. E. Burn, *The Council of Nicaea* [New York: The Macmillan Co., 1925], pp. 5, 56.)

Dr. Burn speaks of the discovery of a papyrus known as No. 1914 in the British Museum in London, England, and dated at about A.D. 335, in which Callistus, a monk of the day, tells of the cruelties of Athanasius, including charges of violence and the use of soldiers to imprison those who opposed him.

H. Idris Bell, editor of the British Museum, writing in *Jews and Christians in Egypt*, and quoted by Burns, says of the conflict between Arius and Athanasius at Nicaea:

"Both sides were tarred with the same brush: the leaders of both were for the most part conspicuously lacking in the virtue of Christian charity towards their opponents." (Burn, *Council*, pp. 62-63.)

The council dragged on for months. It took weeks to get started, so slow were the delegates in arriving. Constantine at first favored the arguments of Athanasius, but later switched over to Arius, and then back again to Athanasius. He couldn't make up his mind.

He was ruthless with his opponents. When some of the bishops opposed him, he promptly banished them, divested them of their ecclesiastical positions and appointed others of his own choosing to succeed them. Inspiration, of course, had nothing to do with it. Neither did divine authority, for Constantine was not so much as a member of the Church in those days.

But he was king! That is what mattered. He had made the Church a department of his government and treated it like the other departments of state, appointing and dismissing his underlings as he pleased. The entire situation was a sad one.

Out of the ancient council came a document of only philosophical thought. Nothing else was possible, considering the two protagonists. And so the scholarly bishops wrote of God in dark and confusing terms like this:

"We worship one God in trinity, and trinity in unity, neither confounding the persons nor dividing the substance. . . . . There are not three incomprehensibles, but one incomprehensible. . . . So the Father is God, the Son is God, and the Holy Ghost is God. Yet they are not three gods but one god. So the Father is Lord, the Son is Lord, and the Holy Ghost is Lord, and yet not three Lords but one Lord. . . . They are not three Almighties but one Almighty. . . . For like as we are compelled by Christian verity to acknowledge every person by himself to be God and Lord, so we are forbidden to say there be three Gods or three Lords."

Is this very different from Plato's definition of God, given four hundred years before Christ? He described the Deity in these words:

"He being the cause of all perceptible things but himself having no color, no shape, no dimension, none of such qualities as may be seen by the eye, but yet is that which exists beyond all existence, unutterable, indescribable, and yet alone beautiful and good." (Hugh Nibley, *The World and the Prophets* [Salt Lake City: Deseret Book Co.], p. 55.)

To further indicate the manner in which pagan thought influenced the Christian view of God at that time, we quote the following from the *Twentieth Century Encyclopedia of Catholicism*:

"What would have happened if St. Athanasius had not made use of Greek thought as well as Scripture? . . .

" 'From the religious point of view, [Christianity] could never have overridden the differences between Greek and Barbarian, Jew and Gentile, if it had remained Jewish in its way of thought, and if it had not acquired, through contact with the Greek genius, that suppleness which enabled it to reach all systems of thought' (Tixeront, *History of Dogma*)."

And again:

"Greek theology was well adapted to become a marvelous guide to express for man . . . the depth of his relationship with God." (*Twentieth Century Encyclopedia of Catholicism*, Vol. 17 [New York: Hawthorn Books, 1958], pp. 118, 123.)

Even further peculiar notions about the Godhead developed as Greek scholars took over the direction of the Church. They continued to argue over the nature of Deity. They did not let the Nicene Creed rest. It was further debated, torn apart, applied locally with alterations in some congregations; some notions were even borrowed from the land of Nirvana and mixed with the doctrines they had evolved.

The creed was tampered with at the Council of Sardica in 343, at the Council of Constantinople in 381, and at the Council of Jerusalem in 381. It was further touched up, mostly for local use, at the Council of Antioch in 375, at the Council of Ephesus in 449 and at the Council of Chalcedon in 451.

The Council of Toledo, Spain, inserted some words which were more to their liking, in 589, as did the Council of Friuli, Italy, in 791. There were other councils, too, some local and some more general, but at each the nature of God was explored, argued and further confused.

Those who say that there was only one united Christian Church in those early days must face the reality of the existence of many sects such as the Arians and Athanasians, who were most prominent at Nicaea, the Anomoeans, the Homoeans, the Eusebians, the Nicaeans, the Meletians, the semi-Arians, the Eustathians, the Alexandrians, and various others. Christianity was anything but united. It was a sad mixture of conflicting groups, each advocating its own views, each one in competition with the others.

It is not surprising then to realize that in fact they knew little or nothing about basic Christianity. They knew less about the Lord whose name they claimed. None of them could give an understandable explanation of his nature.

There was very limited access to scripture, even among the scholars. Holy writ was nonexistent so far as the common people were concerned. Most of them were illiterate anyway.

Many scholars denied the Godhead or Trinity. Others completely depersonalized the Holy Ghost. The creed as written in the fourth century has declared there was a three-in-one God who was admittedly incomprehensible.

In the face of all this, it would have been most refreshing if someone could have read the words of Jesus:

"Learn of me . . . and ye shall find rest unto your souls." (Matthew 11:29.)

But the words were locked away in hidden manuscripts, forbidden to the common people and hardly acknowledged by the philosophers.

The Savior had taught mankind to search the scriptures to learn of his way of life. And why? Because the sacred record revealed his true nature. But it all remained a dark mystery.

Most of the teachers, including Arius and Athanasius, as well as others of the early fathers such as St. Augustine, Origen and Jerome, believed in and taught of a three-in-one God, not three separate Beings. They believed that he was wise and was possessed of great wisdom. This wisdom they called the Son of God! Thus they depersonalized the Savior!

His breath gave life. This breath, they taught, is the Holy Spirit. So they also depersonalized the Holy Ghost. Hence, in their view, there were Father, Son and Holy Ghost, yet they were but one undivided substance. God had wisdom, and this they said was Jesus Christ, the Redeemer. And what of the Holy Ghost?

At one time they declared the Holy Spirit was the breath of God. At another time they taught that the Father and Son loved each other with a holy love, and it was this love which constituted the Holy Spirit.

The *Twentieth Century Encyclopedia of Catholicism*, discusses these doctrines this way:

"St. Augustine . . . departed from the Greek exposition of the subject. . . . Augustine showed that he [the Holy Ghost] proceeds from the Father and Son. . . . — that Father and Son are entranced with love for each other, [that] they meet in a love which is common to both. *That love . . . is the holy spirit."* (*Encyclopedia*, Vol. 17, p. 124. Italics added.)

He also taught that it was God's breath which was breathed into Adam to make him live. This breath was also identified as the Holy Spirit.

In the same book we read: "This . . . love is the Holy Spirit, *of whom Saint Bernard said that he is 'the kiss exchanged between Father and Son,'* " (*Encyclopedia*, Vol. 17, p. 131. Italics added.)

Certainly, God was unknown to them and to all other Christians of that day as well, at least from A.D. 200 onward.

How far they had departed from the true knowledge of God! How lost they were in the dark forest of their imaginations! God an unknown? He most assuredly was to them! They were no closer to an understanding of the Deity than were the Greeks on Mars' Hill to whom Paul preached.

The Greek philosophical influence by now had destroyed the true knowledge and understanding of God for the Christians. It was indeed a dark day.

Philosophy and other secular learning superceded scripture. When the uninspired scholars discovered that they were powerless to properly explain the simple principles of the Christian Godhead, they corrupted it, and made it an intellectual football for continued debate. The general membership of the Church was left in confusion and the truth was buried in deep obscurity.

Chapter Ten

The Mystery Survives

The Athanasian Creed, as amended, was handed down to the time of the Reformers. For most people there was no way of learning the facts about God, since the Bible was not available to them and there was no new revelation.

But the light began to break through the darkness. The Renaissance came. Tyndale, the devoted martyr, Luther, Knox and other brave men did their work. Mankind began to read the scriptures for themselves.

The invention of the printing press, of course, was one of the great blessings which God bestowed upon the world. Several Bible translations appeared in print. With reading came light, and the light showed that current church practices and dogmas were not in harmony with the teachings of holy writ. Hence the Reformation.

But much as it accomplished — and it was much — the Reformation did not restore the true knowledge of God, who continued to be unknown both to lay people and clergy. As Isaiah said, "Darkness shall cover the earth, and gross darkness the people." (Isaiah 60:2.)

Another Paul was needed. A repetition of the episode on Mars' Hill would have brought a great light. But only a partial illumination of truth came at this time.

The Reformation churches continued to grope with regard to the nature of God. They rejoiced in their scriptures, but what of their form of worship? Could anyone worship God intelligently without knowing who or what he is? A true knowledge of Deity was the most pressing need of the world then, just as it is now.

As the Reformers studied holy writ, they nevertheless were blind to the true meaning of things. The scriptures still were a closed book to them in many respects. The clergy were powerless to define Deity.

They were too tightly bound to the creeds of the past. Many wondered and speculated. What was God like? Was he truly one in three and three in one? Was he a Person or merely some essence or influence, or an indescribable, formless, invisible, unknowable mass floating about and filling the immensity of space? They did not know.

The Reformers learned no more about the true nature of God than had Augustine, Origen, Athanasius or Arius. Darkness still prevailed. Because they had nothing better, some of the reformed churches adopted what was left to them from Nicaea, that impossible, uninspired, contradictory and meaningless definition of Deity. So they wrote their own creeds based largely upon it.

One said: "God is an infinite spirit without form or body and is everywhere present."

Another said: "He is an invisible spiritual substance everywhere present at once."

Others:

"He is an infinite spirit everywhere present at the same time, without form, body, parts or passions."

"He is a spirit without body, parts or passions, of incomprehensible shape, everywhere present at once."

"He is a three-in-one Deity as the Nicene Creed sets forth."

One denomination, which is a leader in today's Christianity, said:

"There is no such thing as form or shape connected with God; he is a Spirit without body, parts or passions."

Still another insisted that a three-in-one God permeates the universe, having no definite form or limit. "He is a person and yet not an individual as we know persons, and he is incomprehensible."

And then there was one which said:

"God is universal intelligence, everywhere present, with no form, body or shape." This group believes that at death our intelligence is merged into the universal intelligence, and that constitutes immortality.

So what did they have? A conglomeration of definitions proving that Christians themselves do not all worship the same God. Of what value is faith based on such creeds?

It is to be remembered that the Savior taught that our faith is in vain if we worship him by the precepts of men. Said he: "In vain they do worship me, teaching for doctrines the commandments of men." (Matthew 15:9.)

The new Jerusalem Bible, with the proper imprimatur, gives an interesting rendering of the Savior's teaching on this point.

In Mark 7:6-9, we read these powerful words:

"This people honors me with lip service, while their hearts are far from me. The worship they offer me is worthless: the doctrines they teach are only human regulations."

It then goes on:

"You put aside the commandment of God to cling to human traditions. And he said to them: How ingeniously you get around the commandment of God in order to preserve your tradition. . . . You make God's word null and void for the sake of your tradition which you have handed down. And you do many other things like this."

When the New English Version of the Bible appeared, it carried this rendering of the passage in Matthew: "So by these traditions of yours you have made God's laws ineffectual."

Was tradition involved in the sixteenth-century acceptance of the doctrines of the Nicene Creed? Of course it was, and it cast the Protestants into a gloomy abyss of darkness concerning the divine nature. The confusion of Mars' Hill was still with them.

Chapter Eleven

The Truth Restored

There was no way that mankind could truly worship God if they remained in ignorance of him. The actual knowledge of God must be restored to make worship meaningful.

Jesus had said that if we worship him according to man-made doctrines our worship is in vain. (See Matthew 15:9.) He also stated that we are to learn of him in order to find rest for our souls. (See Matthew 11:29.)

The complete loss of the knowledge of God was a demonstration of the fact of a universal apostasy in the Christian Church, long predicted by the prophets. But the prophets had likewise foretold a universal restoration of "all things which God hath spoken by the mouth of all his holy prophets since the world began." (Acts 3:21.)

That necessarily would include a restoration of the true knowledge of God. This was accomplished in the First Vision of the Prophet Joseph Smith, who saw and communed with God the Eternal Father, and his Beloved Son, Jesus Christ, our Savior and Redeemer.

There he beheld that indeed man is in the form and shape of God, that the Father and Son as separate Beings truly resemble each other and that man resembles them in form and physical likeness.

By modern revelation, confirmed in the Bible, we learn that the Savior had achieved divinity in his preexistence. He was in the beginning with God, and sat at the right hand "of the Majesty on High." (Hebrews 1:1-3.)

But he became flesh and dwelt among us and was known as Jesus of Nazareth whom the prophets said would come into the world. (See John 1:1-14.)

In mortality he descended below all things, only to rise above all things. "He [was] despised and rejected of men; a man of sorrows, and acquainted with grief: and we hid as it were our faces from him." (Isaiah 53:3.)

And yet all power was given him in heaven and in earth. His name was "called Wonderful, Counseller, The mighty God, The everlasting Father, The Prince of Peace." (Isaiah 9:6.)

And his glory was that of the Only Begotten Son of God, who was full of grace and truth. (See John 1:14.)

At his birth the angel said: "Thou shalt call his name Jesus: for he shall *save his people from their sins*." Also: "And they shall call his name Emmanuel, which being interpreted is, *God with us*." (Matthew 1:21-23. Italics added.)

How significant are these scriptures! How little understood!

Being the Savior, Jesus therefore endeavors to bring all mankind unto him.

Since he is no respecter of persons, all who will come may come and receive of his blessings. He offers peace to everyone!

His invitation is clear and warm and forthright: "Come unto me, all ye that labour and are heavy laden, and I will give you rest." (Matthew 11:28.)

The poorest waif, the humblest wage earner, the slave to sin, the discouraged, the downtrodden — whether man, woman, or child — all may come and receive a kind welcome. The rich man, the diplomat, the mighty of the earth may come also if they humble themselves. None will be turned away; all will be blessed if only they will hearken to his voice.

His qualifying requirement, however, must not be overlooked:

"Take my yoke upon you." (Matthew 11:29.) It is a commandment.

What a wealth of purpose is expressed in those few words! But exactly what do they mean? How do we take his yoke upon us? What is a yoke anyway?

Both Greek and Latin derivatives of the word provide the same definition: "To join, to couple, to link; to join together."

In a sense, this is another of the Lord's parables. While on earth, Jesus constantly taught in parables, using terms familiar to his hearers. They understood the language of farming when he gave them the parable of the sower. They knew about plowing and planting and oxen in the mire.

And they knew what a yoke was, and that it coupled together their beasts of burden, permitting the animals to pull side by side, thus bringing their maximum strength to the plow.

With such a simile in mind, he gave this new commandment, which he knew would be of inestimable worth to us if it were followed: to link our strength with his, and his with ours. To take his yoke upon us is a commandment, yes, but also what an invitation to a marvelous opportunity is thus provided — to link his strength to ours!

By what means do we thus "join" with him? How is it accomplished?

We do it by taking upon us his holy name.

"Take upon you the name of Christ," the Lord commands. (D&C 18:21.)

This is vital, but just how is it done?

It is accomplished through sincere conversion followed by the ordinance of baptism, as the Lord himself explains:

"All those who humble themselves before God, and desire to be baptized, and come forth with broken hearts and contrite spirits, and witness before the Church that they have truly repented of all their sins, and are willing to take upon them the name of Jesus Christ, having a determination to serve him to the end, and truly manifest by their works that they have received of the Spirit of Christ unto the remission of their sins, shall be received by baptism into his church." (D&C 20:37.)

That is what it means to take upon us his yoke. That is the way we "join" with Christ.

But this is not all. We further take his yoke upon us by partaking of the emblems of the sacrament of the Lord's Supper. Then, as the prayer indicates, believers "eat in remembrance of the body of thy Son, and witness unto thee, O God, the Eternal Father, that they are willing to take upon them the name of thy Son, and always remember him and keep his commandments which he has given them." (D&C 20:77.)

Then, considering all this, the act of taking upon us the yoke of the Savior is the most serious and solemn thing we can do in life.

Vital as it is, he encourages us by adding that "my yoke is easy, and my burden is light." (Matthew 11:30.)

Easy? Is it easy to keep all of his commandments, and always remember him, and never forget him nor the yoke we have taken upon ourselves?

Easy? Yes, infinitely so, when compared to the staggering weight of sin. And how rewarding it is!

His yoke is uplifting, it is exhilarating, instructive, joyful, and it provides for us the abundant life. Can it possibly be regarded as burdensome?

But if we take his yoke upon us, we must understand that we are not to treat it lightly. Rather, we are to "seek . . . first the kingdom of God, and his righteousness." (Matthew 6:33.) We must serve him with all our "heart, might, mind and strength" (D&C 4:2), and we must have an eye single to his glory. If we fail in this, we jeopardize the promise. (D&C 82:10.)

We must never trifle with sacred things (see D&C 6:12), for God will not be mocked (see D&C 104:6). There is no place for hypocrisy.

One of the great truths the Lord gave early in his ministry is this: "No man can serve two masters. . . . Ye cannot serve God and mammon." (Matthew 6:24.)

Sincerity, devotion, honesty of purpose — these are required of all who take his yoke upon them. We must continue to live *in* the world, of course, because that is part of mortal experience, but we are not to be *of* the world.

To take his yoke upon us includes also what Peter had in mind when he declared that we shall be "a chosen generation, a royal priesthood, an holy nation, a peculiar people; that ye should shew forth the praises of him who hath called you out of darkness into his marvellous light." (1 Peter 2:9.)

Chapter Twelve

"... Learn of Me"

The Savior expects intelligent worship from his followers. He teaches that the glory of God is intelligence, and it must be the glory of man also.

Therefore, as we take upon us his yoke, he commands: "Learn of me." (Matthew 11:29.)

It is as much a commandment as any of the others he has given us. It is the key to progress in his Church, for no one can be saved in ignorance. (See D&C 131:6.)

But how are we to learn of him? Can we, by searching, find out God?

The answer is yes, a thousand times yes. It *is* the way to find him. We must seek and we must ask; we must knock at the door, and if we do so in all earnestness, we shall surely find. And just as surely we shall receive, and the door will be opened to us, for such is the Lord's promise.

The early members of our Church were a humble and a contrite group. They earnestly desired to know his will, that they might better serve him. He spoke to them in plainness, but in loving terms, and said:

"Verily I say unto you, my friends, I leave these sayings with you to ponder in your hearts, with this commandment which I give unto you, that ye shall call upon me while I am near —

"Draw near to me and I will draw near unto you; seek me diligently and ye shall find me; ask, and ye shall receive; knock, and it shall be opened unto you.

"Whatsoever ye ask the Father in my name it shall be given unto you, that is expedient for you.

"And if ye ask anything that is not expedient for you, it shall turn unto your condemnation.

"Behold, that which you hear is as the voice of one crying in the wilderness — in the wilderness, because you cannot see him — my voice, because my voice is Spirit; my Spirit is truth; truth abideth and hath no end; and if it be in you it shall abound.

"And if your eye be single to my glory, your whole bodies shall be filled with light, and there shall be no darkness in you; and that body which is filled with light comprehendeth all things.

"Therefore, sanctify yourselves that your minds become single to God, and the days will come that you shall see him; for he will unveil his face unto you, and it shall be in his own time, and his own way, and according to his own will." (D&C 88:62-68.)

Then how shall we seek him? By prayer, by study, and by faith; by righteous living, and by casting away idle thoughts and excess laughter; by seeking first the kingdom of God and his righteousness; by searching the scriptures, "for they are they which testify of me." (John 5:39; see also D&C 88; 109.)

The "best books" will become our libraries. Sincere prayer will bring us answers with great growth in spirituality. Our chapels will be spiritual schoolhouses wherein we may both learn and worship; our temples will be seen as places of sacred instruction, and our homes also may become such for our families.

So, indeed, to find God — to learn of the Savior — we must seek him, and do so diligently. As we seek his kingdom, we also must help to build it by our earnest labors.

Let us remember that if we seek not, we find not. But find him we must, for our very salvation depends upon it.

Said the Lord to the Prophet Joseph Smith: "Jesus Christ is the name which is given of the Father, and there is none other name given whereby men can be saved;

"Wherefore, all men must take upon them the name which is given of the Father, for in that name shall they be called at the last day;

"Wherefore, if they know not the name by which they are called, they cannot have place in the kingdom of my Father." (D&C 18:23-25.)

Jesus was always approachable. He was so in mortality, and is likewise today.

When Jairus needed help, it was given him. When the adulterous woman was thrust into his presence, she did not suffer condemnation, but received pity and kindness instead. When the woman with the issue of blood touched the hem of his garment and was healed, there was no censure, only commendation for her faith. When the importunate woman persisted in seeking a blessing, in full compassion it was given her.

There was, however, one great common denominator among them all. Jesus was the Son of God. His followers had to accept that fact or they were not true believers. And that principle must ever be. We, too, must embrace it.

Chapter Thirteen

"I Am He"

In his mortal ministry Jesus announced to an unbelieving, even hostile, world that he was the Son of God. Many who heard him accused him of blasphemy and sought his life, but others believed and followed him.

He spoke lovingly and reverently of the Almighty as his Father, and taught that his gospel really centered in the Father. Always he placed the Father in a position of priority.

When he taught us to pray, he said we must pray to the Father, and added that the Father will hear sincere and earnest supplications. He said that when we pray in secret our Father will reward us openly. He indicated that if we are forgiving in our dealings with other people, the Father will forgive us of our transgressions. (See Matthew 6.) The kingdom of God, he said, is the "kingdom of my Father."

Whenever Jesus announced himself as the Son of the Eternal Father, he did so with the greatest of humility. He did not flaunt his identity before men. As he humbly acknowledged his true and sacred relationship with the Father, it was usually expressed to others who were also humble.

He talked with the Samaritan woman at the well. She had said, "I know that Messias cometh, which is called Christ: when he is come, he will tell us all things."

To this the Master said humbly: "I that speak unto thee am he." (John 4:25-26.)

Think of the circumstances of his thus revealing himself to her. The Jews traditionally "had no dealings with the Samaritans," and yet, here he was, speaking to a Samaritan woman. He knew her to be living with a man to whom she was not married; a woman, too, who had had five husbands previously.

Yet to her he preached his gospel. Even her soul might be saved, and possibly others in her community. So there at the well, apparently with no one else near enough to hear, he told her the significant and striking fact: "I that speak unto thee am he."

To tell this great truth to such a woman, under circumstances like those, certainly required divine humility.

"And many of the Samaritans of that city believed on him for the saying of the woman, which testified, He told me all that ever I did.

"So when the Samaritans were come unto him, they besought him that he would tarry with them: and he abode there two days.

"And many more believed because of his own word;

"And said unto the woman, Now we believe, not because of thy saying: for we have heard him ourselves, and know that this is indeed the Christ, the Saviour of the world." (John 4:39-42.)

How often as he healed people did he humbly say, "Tell no man!"? Some of them, at the time, evidently did not know who he was, but they must have known afterward. It was necessary to their salvation, for only in his name could they be saved.

Even in Gethsemane he left no doubt about himself. This was a most touching incident, but one which taught a great lesson. The crucifiers had their Judas, it is true, and he gave the betrayal kiss. But still Jesus left no question in their minds. His true identity must be known, even to them, for a just judgment must come to them.

As they approached him, the scriptures say that the Lord

"went forth" to meet them, "and said unto them, Whom seek ye?

"They answered him, Jesus of Nazareth. Jesus saith unto them, I am he." (John 18:4-5.)

So even the crucifiers had it made plain to them.

The high priest who brought about the Crucifixion was not left in darkness either. Jesus personally saw to that. This arrogant religious bigot "asked him, and said unto him, Art thou the Christ, the Son of the Blessed? And Jesus said, I am." (Mark 14:61-62.)

It was likewise with Pilate, who cannot escape blame for his part in the Crucifixion.

"Pilate asked him, Art thou the King of the Jews? And he answering said unto him, Thou sayest it." (Mark 15:2.) Or as we would say in modern terms, "You have spoken correctly."

When Pilate confronted the hostile high priests who wanted him to release Barabbas instead of Christ, he said: "What will ye then that I shall do unto him whom ye call the King of the Jews?" It was then that these hypocritical clerics cried out, "Crucify him." (Mark 15:12-13.)

And when Pilate followed their bidding, he placed above the cross the very identification which condemned both himself and them: "The King of the Jews."

The crucifiers indeed knew who he was. They were without excuse. Pilate was a Roman, and apparently acted out of fear of the crowds. But not so the high priests. They knew the scriptures, and those sacred works testified of Christ. (See John 5:39.)

But the Lord made it clear even to Pilate, the pagan. Note this passage from John's gospel:

"Then Pilate entered into the judgment hall again, and called Jesus, and said unto him, Art thou the King of the Jews?

"Jesus answered him, Sayest thou this thing of thyself, or did others tell it thee of me?

"Pilate answered, Am I a Jew? Thine own nation and the chief priests have delivered thee unto me: what hast thou done?

"Jesus answered, My kingdom is not of this world: if my kingdom were of this world, then would my servants fight, that I should not be delivered to the Jews: but now is my kingdom not from hence.

"Pilate therefore said unto him, Art thou a king then? Jesus answered, Thou sayest that I am a king. To this end was I born, and for this cause came I into the world, that I should bear witness unto the truth. Every one that is of the truth heareth my voice.

"Pilate saith unto him, what is truth? And when he had said this, he went out again unto the Jews, and saith unto them, I find in him no fault at all.

"But ye have a custom, that I should release unto you one at the passover: will ye therefore that I release unto you the King of the Jews?

"Then cried they all again, saying, Not this man, but Barabbas. Now Barabbas was a robber." (John 18:33-40.)

And then again John wrote:

"Then Pilate therefore took Jesus, and scourged him.

"And the soldiers platted a crown of thorns, and put it on his head, and they put on him a purple robe.

"And said, Hail, King of the Jews! and they smote him with their hands.

"Pilate therefore went forth again, and saith unto them, Behold, I bring him forth to you, that ye may know that I find no fault in him.

"Then came Jesus forth, wearing the crown of thorns, and the purple robe. And Pilate saith unto them, Behold the man!

"When the chief priests therefore and officers saw him, they cried out, saying, Crucify him, crucify him. Pilate saith unto them, Take ye him, and crucify him: for I find no fault in him.

"The Jews answered him, We have a law, and by our law he ought to die, because he made himself the Son of God.

"When Pilate therefore heard that saying, he was the more afraid;

"And went again into the judgment hall, and saith unto Jesus, Whence art thou? But Jesus gave him no answer.

"Then saith Pilate unto him, Speakest thou not unto me?

knowest thou not that I have power to crucify thee, and have power to release thee?

"Jesus answered, Thou couldest have no power at all against me, except it were given thee from above: therefore he that delivered me unto thee hath the greater sin.

"And from thenceforth Pilate sought to release him: but the Jews cried out, saying, If thou let this man go, thou art not Caesar's friend: whosoever maketh himself a king speaketh against Caesar.

"When Pilate therefore heard that saying, he brought Jesus forth, and sat down in the judgment seat in a place that is called the Pavement, but in the Hebrew, Gabbatha.

"And it was the preparation of the passover, and about the sixth hour: and he saith unto the Jews, Behold your King!

"But they cried out, Away with him, away with him, crucify him. Pilate saith unto them, Shall I crucify your King? The chief priests answered, We have no king but Caesar.

"Then delivered he him therefore unto them to be crucified. And they took Jesus, and led him away.

"And he bearing his cross went forth into a place called the place of a skull, which is called in the Hebrew Golgotha:

"Where they crucified him, and two other with him, on either side one, and Jesus in the midst.

"And Pilate wrote a title, and put it on the cross. And the writing was, JESUS OF NAZARETH THE KING OF THE JEWS.

"This title then read many of the Jews: for the place where Jesus was crucified was nigh to the city: and it was written in Hebrew, and Greek, and Latin.

"Then said the chief priests of the Jews to Pilate, Write not, The King of the Jews; but that he said, I am King of the Jews.

"Pilate answered, What I have written I have written." (John 19:1-22.)

The Roman centurion who saw him die on the cross likewise was convinced, and said, "Truly this man was the Son of God." (Mark 15:39.) Heaven had sent an earthquake, and such a sign the centurion could well understand. (See Matthew 27:54.)

Not only was his identification made known to the humble during his ministry and at the time of his death, but it was so at his resurrection as well.

When the angel came to make the announcement of his rising from the tomb, it was to humble, grieving women that he spoke: "I know that ye seek Jesus which was crucified. He is not here: for he is risen." (Matthew 28:5-6.)

The Lord's first appearance as a resurrected being was not to a multitude, nor to the world at large, nor even to his chosen eleven disciples. It was to weeping Mary that he made himself known. (See John 20:16-18.)

With such humility on his part, is it any wonder that he commanded that his followers must become as humble as a little child? (See Matthew 18:1-6.)

Having meekly but so surely identified himself, his disciples were deeply impressed, and received such a great conviction in their own hearts that they were able to testify of him to "all the world" as Jesus had commanded them.

Being given the power of the Holy Ghost, they did so in great plainness and with tremendous courage.

When Peter addressed the curious crowd in the temples, he upbraided them and said:

"Ye denied the Holy One and the Just, and desired a murderer to be granted unto you; And killed the Prince of life, whom God hath raised from the dead; whereof we are witnesses." (Acts 3:14.)

When he and John were called into question by the authorities, they cried out: "Whether it be right in the sight of God to hearken unto you more than unto God, judge ye." (Acts 4:19.)

They prayed: "And now, Lord, behold their threatenings: and grant unto thy servants that with all boldness they may speak thy word,

"By stretching forth thine hand to heal; and that signs and wonders may be done by the name of thy holy child Jesus." (Acts 4:29-30.)

Then the scripture goes on to say:

"When they had prayed, the place was shaken where they were assembled together; and they were all filled with the Holy Ghost, and they spake the word of God with bold-ness." (Acts 4:31.)

And further:

"And with great power gave the apostles witness of the resurrection of the Lord Jesus: and great grace was upon them all." (Acts 4:33.)

As he introduced himself to the Nephites following his resurrection in Palestine, he brought startling and convincing certainty to "his other sheep."

Storms, earthquakes, and fires had riddled their land for three days, and they were testimonies that could not be mis-understood. Then, as calm came, the Lord descended from the skies, introduced again by his Eternal Father, and said to the people:

"I am Jesus Christ, whom the prophets testified shall come into the world." (3 Nephi 11:10.)

A multitude of twenty-five hundred people fell down and worshipped him. Then, one by one, they came up at his invitation and examined the marks of the Crucifixion, and knew for a certainty that he was indeed the Christ, the Son of God. There was no doubt among them about his true identity!

When he stood before Joseph Smith and Oliver Cowdery in the Kirtland Temple, there was the same certainty of iden-tification. There, as they looked upon him, he said:

"I am the first and the last; I am he who liveth, I am he who was slain; I am your advocate with the Father." (D&C 110:4.)

They saw him clearly and wrote a description of his appearance. They heard his voice, too, which "was as the sound of the rushing of great waters, even the voice of Jehovah." (D&C 110:3.)

And when Joseph Smith and Sidney Rigdon were given their view of the heavens, and beheld the Savior on the right hand of God, with the holy angels, they heard the voice "bearing record that he is the Only Begotten of the Father — That by him, and through him, and of him, the worlds are and were created." (D&C 76:23-24.) There was no room for doubt.

As the Lord gave other revelations to the Prophet Joseph Smith, instructing him in the manner of setting up the latter-day kingdom, he repeatedly identified himself, not now as the lowly preacher of Palestine, but as the Mighty God, the Alpha and the Omega, Jesus the Savior — Christ the Lord!

So in our day he speaks as the glorified Redeemer to whom all power has been given in heaven and in earth. It is this Deity — this Christ — to whom we must account for the deeds done in the flesh.

Indeed, as he himself said: "I am he!"

Chapter Fourteen

Angels and Devils Knew Him

The Father testified of Jesus, both at his baptism and at the Transfiguration. In each case he declared: "Thou art my beloved Son," or "This is my beloved Son." (Matthew 3:17; Mark 1:11; Luke 9:35; 2 Peter 1:17.)

The Savior continually testified of himself. The Jews sought to kill him because he affirmed that he was the Son of God. (See John 5:18.) Obviously he told them plainly, since they were so angry that they sought to take his life.

Both angels and devils also testified of him. No one was given any excuse for not knowing him, for they were told repeatedly in testimonies vocally expressed in various ways. And in addition to all of that, the ancient prophets — in the scriptures which the people of Palestine possessed and pretended to believe — testified of him. So angels, prophets, and devils all knew him.

Luke records one important instance of the testimony of devils:

"Now when the sun was setting, all they that had any sick with divers diseases brought them unto him; and he laid his hands on every one of them, and healed them.

"And the devils also came out of many, crying out, and saying, Thou art Christ the Son of God. And he rebuking them suffered them not to speak: for they knew that he was Christ." (Luke 4:40-41.)

Again we have this:

"And in the synagogue there was a man, which had a spirit of an unclean devil, and cried out with a loud voice,

"Saying, Let us alone; what have we to do with thee, thou Jesus of Nazareth? art thou come to destroy us? I know thee who thou art; the Holy One of God." (Luke 4:33-34.)

And Matthew records:

"And when he was come to the other side into the country of the Gergesenes, there met him two possessed with devils, coming out of the tombs, exceeding fierce, so that no man might pass by that way.

"And, behold, they cried out, saying, What have we to do with thee, Jesus, thou Son of God? art thou come hither to torment us before the time?" (Matthew 8:28-29.)

Mark gives us more examples:

"And there was in their synagogue a man with an unclean spirit; and he cried out,

"Saying, Let us alone; what have we to do with thee, thou Jesus of Nazareth? art thou come to destroy us? I know thee who thou art, the Holy One of God.

"And Jesus rebuked him, saying, Hold thy peace, and come out of him.

"And when the unclean spirit had torn him, and cried with a loud voice, he came out of him." (Mark 1:23-26.)

Another instance is provided by this same writer:

"And he healed many that were sick of divers diseases, and cast out many devils; and suffered not the devils to speak, because they knew him." (Mark 1:34.)

Mark also tells us this:

"And unclean spirits, when they saw him, fell down before him, and cried, saying, Thou art the Son of God." (Mark 3:11.)

Apparently the Lord did not relish the intrusion of the testimonies of these wicked devils, for in virtually every case where they testified, he instructed them to "not make him known." (Mark 3:12.) Nevertheless, they knew!

Of course, the greatest testimony from the lower regions

came from Lucifer himself, who challenged the Savior with his "If thou be the Son of God" insults, and his repeated temptations.

This archdemon was known as Lucifer in the preexistence, and once had been an angel of great authority in the presence of God. Because of his wickedness he became Satan, "that old serpent, even the devil, who rebelled against God, and sought to take the kingdom of our God and his Christ —

"Wherefore, he maketh war with the saints of God, and encompasseth them around about." (D&C 76:28-29.)

Satan's efforts, of course, were no temptation to the Master, because Jesus had known Lucifer in the preexistence and could see through his every device. He had seen his challenge to the Eternal Father when the plan of salvation was presented and knew of his ambitious demands. He had seen Michael the archangel and his armies drive Lucifer from the courts on high, together with the hosts who followed him, and had seen them thrust down to the earth.

So the Savior knew exactly whom he was dealing with, knew all about his wiles and deceptions. There was no way in which Lucifer could really tempt him. The Lord must have been filled with utter disgust that Lucifer would have the effrontery to assail him, especially now, when he was completing a forty-day fast.

Though the Lord may have been weak physically from his long abstinence from food, there certainly was no weakness in his spirit nor in his perception. "Get thee hence, Satan," was his response. "Thou shalt worship the Lord thy God, and him only shalt thou serve." (Matthew 4:10.)

Jesus in the preexistence was Jehovah, and had achieved divinity there. He was the Firstborn of the Father and, as John said, "The Word was God." (John 1:1.)

Lucifer, on the other hand, had become the devil, thereby taking a completely opposite course from that chosen by the Savior. What a contrast in behavior! Jesus by obedience became divine; Lucifer by disobedience became the devil. Our own crossroads are not so different.

So, it was altogether appropriate that Jesus, during these temptations, said to Satan: "Thou shalt not tempt the Lord thy God." (Matthew 4:7.) Jesus was the Lord God — and Lucifer knew it.

It is significant that angels came and ministered to Jesus following this encounter with Lucifer. The angels knew the facts in the case. From the presence of God in heaven they had come to further sustain their Savior and ours.

All the hosts of heaven knew him. Had they not sung at his birth?

The herald angel on that first Christmas announced: "I bring you good tidings of great joy, which shall be to all people. For unto you is born this day in the city of David a Saviour, which is Christ the Lord." (Luke 2:10-11.)

When the Annunciation was made to Mary, the angel declared that her child would be the "Son of the Highest," therefore "that holy thing which shall be born of thee shall be called the Son of God." (Luke 1:32, 35.)

He was to be called Jesus, that name meaning "the Savior." (Matthew 1:21.) To make it fully clear that he was divine, a thing which Mary must know, the angel said the babe also was to be called Emmanuel, "which being interpreted is, God with us." (Matthew 1:23.) "And the Word was God." (John 1:1.)

The wise men believed that he was the King of kings, for they understood the scriptures. They knew, too, that a star would lead them to the Holy Child. To them it was his star. When they saw him, they fell down and worshipped him, and gave him their precious gifts. They recognized him without question.

Was anyone left in doubt about his divine identity? Did anyone have excuse?

Chapter Fifteen

Ancient Prophets Spoke

From the very beginning the prophets testified of Christ. They told where he would be born, what his mission was, that his mother would be a virgin, and that he would come to save his people from their sins.

They declared that he would be a man of sorrows and acquainted with grief, that people would see no beauty in him that would make him seem desirable to them; that when brought to judgment he would "openeth not his mouth" (Isaiah 53); that "his name shall be called Wonderful, Counseller, The mighty God, The everlasting Father, The Prince of Peace." (Isaiah 9:6.)

The predictions of the past were so plain that even the wise men of the East — apparently non-Jewish — recognized the signs of his birth, and followed his promised star to the place where the Holy Child lay, and there they worshipped him.

With the scriptures being so clear, must not the scribes, the elders and the high priests, who were the scriptural experts of the day, also have known? But they had blinded themselves by their traditions and by their love for doctrines of their own manufacture. Their own selfish prejudices forced them to reject him.

Jesus taught us to search the scriptures, for "they are they which testify of me." (John 5:39.)

Moses testified of Christ. It is true that his writings now in the Old Testament are not complete, and obviously do not contain the references Jesus had in mind when he said, "For had ye believed Moses, ye would have believed me: for he wrote of me." (John 5:46.)

The Savior then added: "But if ye believe not his writings, how shall ye believe my words?" (John 5:47.)

It is most interesting to read the following scripture in this connection:

"The day following Jesus would go forth into Galilee, and findeth Philip, and saith unto him, Follow me.

"Now Philip was of Bethsaida, the city of Andrew and Peter.

"Philip findeth Nathanael, and saith unto him, We have found him, of whom Moses in the law, and the prophets, did write, Jesus of Nazareth, the son of Joseph." (John 1:43-45.)

After the resurrection of the Lord, he walked toward Emmaus with two disciples who told him of the Crucifixion, not recognizing him. Then the Lord "saith unto them, O fools, and slow of heart to believe all that the prophets have spoken:

"Ought not Christ to have suffered these things, and to enter into his glory?

"And beginning at Moses and all the prophets, he expounded unto them in all the scriptures the things concerning himself." (Luke 24:25-27.)

When Peter preached in the temple to the crowds which assembled following his healing of the crippled man, he said:

"Yea, and all the prophets from Samuel and those that follow after, as many as have spoken, have likewise foretold of these days." (Acts 3:24.)

When Peter preached to Cornelius, the righteous gentile, he said:

"To him give all the prophets witness, that through his name whosoever believeth in him shall receive remission of sins." (Acts 10:43.)

And when Paul, a prisoner in Rome, preached to all who

would come to his house, "he expounded and testified the kingdom of God, persuading them concerning Jesus, both out of the law of Moses and out of the prophets, from morning till evening." (Acts 28:23.)

Of course the scriptures of that day testified of him. Of course Moses wrote of him. Of course the other prophets gave their testimonies.

The Book of Mormon is enlightening in this respect.

Note this from the book of Jacob:

"And I said unto him: Believest thou the scriptures? And he said, Yea.

"And I said unto him: Then ye do not understand them; for they truly testify of Christ. Behold, I say unto you that none of the prophets have written, nor prophesied, save they have spoken concerning this Christ." (Jacob 7:10-11.)

A few of these ancient prophets — their writings obviously being in the brass plates of Laban — are mentioned in the Book of Mormon. Not only are their names given, but declarations they themselves made concerning the Christ are included. Note the following, for example:

"And the God of our fathers, who were led out of Egypt, out of bondage, and also were preserved in the wilderness by him, yea, the God of Abraham, and of Isaac, and the God of Jacob, yieldeth himself, according to the words of the angel, as a man, into the hands of wicked men, to be lifted up, according to the words of Zenock, and to be crucified, according to the words of Neum, and to be buried in a sepulchre, according to the words of Zenos, which he spake concerning the three days of darkness, which should be a sign given of his death unto those who should inhabit the isles of the sea, more especially given unto those who are of the house of Israel.

"For thus spake the prophet: The Lord God surely shall visit all the house of Israel at that day, some with his voice, because of their righteousness, unto their great joy and salvation, and others with the thunderings and the lightnings of his power, by tempest, by fire, and by smoke, and vapor of darkness, and by the opening of the earth, and by mountains which shall be carried up.

"And all these things must surely come, saith the prophet Zenos. And the rocks of the earth must rend; and because of the groanings of the earth, many of the kings of the isles of the sea shall be wrought upon by the Spirit of God, to exclaim: The God of nature suffers.

"And as for those who are at Jerusalem, saith the prophet, they shall be scourged by all people, because they crucify the God of Israel, and turn their hearts aside, rejecting signs and wonders, and the power and glory of the God of Israel.

"And because they turn their hearts aside, saith the prophet, and have despised the Holy One of Israel, they shall wander in the flesh, and perish, and become a hiss and a by-word, and be hated among all nations.

"Nevertheless, when that day cometh, saith the prophet, that they no more turn aside their hearts against the Holy One of Israel, then will he remember the covenants which he made to their fathers.

"Yea, then will he remember the isles of the sea; yea, and all the people who are of the house of Israel, will I gather in, saith the Lord, according to the words of the prophet Zenos, from the four quarters of the earth.

"Yea, and all the earth shall see the salvation of the Lord, saith the prophet; every nation, kindred, tongue and people shall be blessed." (1 Nephi 19:10-17.)

Speaking of the writings of Moses which testify of Christ, many of them are provided by the Prophet Joseph Smith as we have them in the book of Moses in the Pearl of Great Price.

For example, he gave us this by revelation:

"The words of God, which he spake unto Moses at a time when Moses was caught up into an exceedingly high mountain,

"And he saw God face to face, and he talked with him, and the glory of God was upon Moses; therefore Moses could endure his presence.

"And God spake unto Moses, saying: Behold, I am the Lord God Almighty, and Endless is my name; for I am without beginning of days or end of years; and is not this endless?

"And, behold, thou art my son; wherefore look, and I will show thee the workmanship of mine hands; but not all, for my works are without end, and also my words, for they never cease.

"Wherefore, no man can behold all my works, except he behold all my glory; and no man can behold all my glory, and afterwards remain in the flesh on the earth.

"And I have work for thee, Moses, my son; and thou art in the similitude of mine Only Begotten; and mine Only Begotten is and shall be the Savior, for he is full of grace and truth; but there is no God beside me, and all things are present with me, for I know them all.

"And now, behold, this one thing I show unto thee, Moses, my son; for thou art in the world, and now I show it unto thee.

"And it came to pass that Moses looked, and beheld the world upon which he was created; and Moses beheld the world and the ends thereof, and all the children of men which are, and which were created; of the same he greatly marveled and wondered.

"And the presence of God withdrew from Moses, that his glory was not upon Moses; and Moses was left unto himself. And as he was left unto himself, he fell unto the earth.

"And it came to pass that it was for the space of many hours before Moses did again receive his natural strength like unto man; and he said unto himself: Now, for this cause I know that man is nothing, which thing I never had supposed.

"But now mine own eyes have beheld God; but not my natural, but my spiritual eyes, for my natural eyes could not have beheld; for I should have withered and died in his presence; but his glory was upon me; and I beheld his face, for I was transfigured before him.

"And it came to pass that when Moses had said these words, behold, Satan came tempting him, saying: Moses, son of man, worship me.

"And it came to pass that Moses looked upon Satan and said: Who art thou? For behold, I am a son of God, in the similitude of his Only Begotten; and where is thy glory, that I should worship thee?

"For behold, I could not look upon God, except his glory

should come upon me, and I were strengthened before him. But I can look upon thee in the natural man. Is it not so, surely?

"Blessed be the name of my God, for his Spirit hath not altogether withdrawn from me, or else where is thy glory, for it is darkness unto me? And I can judge between thee and God; for God said unto me: Worship God, for him only shalt thou serve.

"Get thee hence, Satan; deceive me not; for God said unto me: Thou art after the similitude of mine Only Begotten.

"And he also gave me commandments when he called unto me out of the burning bush, saying: Call upon God in the name of mine Only Begotten, and worship me.

"And again Moses said: I will not cease to call upon God, I have other things to inquire of him: for his glory has been upon me, wherefore I can judge between him and thee. Depart hence, Satan.

"And now, when Moses had said these words, Satan cried with a loud voice, and rent upon the earth, and commanded, saying: I am the Only Begotten, worship me.

"And it came to pass that Moses began to fear exceedingly; and as he began to fear, he saw the bitterness of hell. Nevertheless, calling upon God, he received strength, and he commanded, saying: Depart from me Satan, for this one God only will I worship, which is the God of glory.

"And now Satan began to tremble, and the earth shook; and Moses received strength, and called upon God, saying: In the name of the Only Begotten, depart hence, Satan.

"And it came to pass that Satan cried with a loud voice, with weeping, and wailing, and gnashing of teeth; and he departed hence, even from the presence of Moses, that he beheld him not." (Moses 1:1-22.)

Moses was told also that the Savior is the Creator, and that all the worlds were made by him. (See Moses 1:31-33.)

But one of the most impressive of all of Moses' writings is found in his record of the selection of Jehovah as the Savior in our preexistent life. Moses wrote this:

"And I, the Lord God, spake unto Moses, saying: That Satan, whom thou hast commanded in the name of mine

Only Begotten, is the same which was from the beginning, and he came before me, saying — Behold, here am I, send me, I will be thy son, and I will redeem all mankind, that one soul shall not be lost, and surely I will do it; wherefore give me thine honor.

"But behold, my Beloved Son, which was my Beloved and Chosen from the beginning, said unto me — Father, thy will be done, and the glory be thine forever.

"Wherefore, because that Satan rebelled against me, and sought to destroy the agency of man, which I, the Lord God, had given him, and also, that I should give unto him mine own power; by the power of mine Only Begotten, I caused that he should be cast down;

"And he became Satan, yea, even the devil, the father of all lies, to deceive and to blind men, and to lead them captive at his will, even as many as would not hearken unto my voice." (Moses 4:1-4.)

Since Jesus spoke so emphatically about the writings of Moses, and quoted them to prove his own identity, were not his more detailed writings available to the people of that day?

Jesus would not have condemned the people if they had not possessed them. He would not have rebuked them for failing to read scriptures which were not available to them.

It is well to remember Nephi's description of the scriptures after they had gone through unhallowed hands. Many "plain and precious things" were taken away "which were plain to the understanding of the children of men, according to the plainness which is in the Lamb of God — because of these things which are taken away out of the gospel of the Lamb, an exceeding great many do stumble, yea, insomuch that Satan hath great power over them." (1 Nephi 13:29.)

That is why these writings are not in our Old Testament. Yet they obviously were available in the day in which Christ lived. He was well identified.

Chapter Sixteen

Divine Father and Son

One of the great lessons which Jesus taught at the very beginning of the history of his modern Church was that we must have an eye single to the work and glory of God.

As he taught our early brethren the qualifications required for service in his kingdom, he said: "Faith, hope, charity and love, with an eye single to the glory of God, qualify him for the work." (D&C 4:5.)

He then followed with this instruction: "Therefore, sanctify yourselves that your minds become single to God." (D&C 88:68.)

There can be no success in the work of the Lord without such devotion, and this Jesus exemplified in every phase of his own experience.

He did so in his preexistent state; he constantly honored his Father during his mortal life; after his resurrection, he did so both in Palestine and in ancient America; and he now continues so to do in his modern ministry.

We must follow this example if we are to be acceptable to him.

In the primeval council in heaven, as he was chosen to become the Savior, he said: "Father, thy will be done, and the glory be thine forever." (Moses 4:2.)

In his dealings with the Nephites, long before he was born in the flesh, he repeatedly referred to his Father, giving to him all glory and honor in everything, and directing the attention of the Nephites to the Father.

Five hundred years before the coming of the Lord, Jacob was taught to pray to the Eternal Father, as all followers of Christ have been instructed to do. (See Jacob 7:22.)

During that same period the prophet Enos, approaching his death, wrote:

"I soon go to the place of my rest, which is with my Redeemer; for I know that in him I shall rest. And I rejoice in the day when my mortal shall put on immortality, and shall stand before him; then shall I see his face with pleasure, and he will say unto me: Come unto me, ye blessed, there is a place prepared for you in the mansions of my Father." (Enos 1:27.)

Half a millennium before the birth of the Savior, Nephi, speaking of the redemption of the Jews, said: "When that day shall come that they shall believe in Christ, and worship the Father in his name, with pure hearts and clean hands, and look not forward any more for another Messiah. . . ." (2 Nephi 25:16.)

In the same discourse Nephi spoke of Jesus as the "Only Begotten of the Father." (2 Nephi 25:12.)

In further reference to the Savior, Nephi referred to him as the "Lamb of God" who "humbleth himself before the Father, and witnesseth unto the Father that he would be obedient unto him in keeping his commandments." (2 Nephi 31:6-7.)

And then he asked, "Wherefore, my beloved brethren, can we follow Jesus save we shall be willing to keep the commandments of the Father?

"And the Father said: Repent ye, repent ye, and be baptized in the name of my Beloved Son."

And then Nephi records:

"The voice of the Son came unto me, saying: He that is baptized in my name, to him will the Father give the Holy Ghost, like unto me; wherefore, follow me, and do the things which ye have seen me do." (1 Nephi 31:10-12.)

Nephi also said, again some five hundred years before the Lord's birth, "And now, behold, this is the doctrine of Christ, and the only and true doctrine of the Father, and of the Son, and of the Holy Ghost." (2 Nephi 31:21.)

It is most interesting that Nephi also said: "Ye must pray always, and not faint; that ye must not perform any thing unto the Lord save in the first place ye shall pray unto the Father in the name of Christ, that he will consecrate thy performance unto thee, that thy performance may be for the welfare of thy soul." (2 Nephi 32:9.)

In the days of Mosiah, about 150 B.C., the same doctrine was taught. When Abinadi talked of Jesus, he said: "Because he dwelleth in the flesh he shall be called the Son of God, having subjected the flesh to the will of the father, . . .

"Even so he shall be led, crucified, and slain, the flesh becoming subject even unto death, the will of the Son being swallowed up in the will of the Father." (Mosiah 15:2, 7.)

How could these prophets speak in this manner, so far in advance of the birth of Jesus?

It was because the premortal Lord himself had so taught them. The gospel in its simplicity and truth was given to the Nephites even though they still lived also under the law of Moses, which was required until the law was fulfilled by the atonement of the Savior.

The proper relationship of the Father was thus made clear to them. Salvation centers in the Father, but comes to us through the ministry of the Savior. Father and Son are in full harmony. Therefore, they are united as one — in one Godhead — as Abinadi taught so plainly. And all of this was because Jesus himself gave all honor and glory to the Father, and did not assume any priority for himself.

Among our friends, we often speak of two or more people being united in thought, intentions and efforts. We say they are of one mind. It is in this manner that God and Christ are one — one in purpose, thought and action.

The Savior's constant deference to the Father is evident all through the New Testament. The Sermon on the Mount is an excellent example.

He taught us to pray to the Father, explained that forgiveness comes from the Father, declared repeatedly that he had been sent from the Father to come into the world, and would return to the Father upon the completion of his mission.

John wrote this:

"And the Father himself, which hath sent me, hath borne witness of me. Ye have neither heard his voice at any time, nor seen his shape.

"And ye have not his word abiding in you: for whom he hath sent, him ye believe not. . . .

"I am come in my Father's name, and ye receive me not: if another shall come in his own name, him ye will receive." (John 5:37-38,43.)

In his crucifixion he himself prayed to the Father, once to seek forgiveness for those who were taking his life, saying, "Father, forgive them; for they know not what they do" (Luke 23:34), and again just before he expired. (See Matthew 27:46 and Luke 23:46.)

Immediately after his resurrection, he again referred to the directing power of the Father. As he met Mary in the garden, and she attempted to touch him, he said: "Touch me not; for I am not yet ascended to my Father: but go to my brethren, and say unto them, I ascend unto my Father, and your Father, and to my God, and your God." (John 20:17.)

Always the Father was the center of the Savior's life and of all that he did in his ministry. Always he taught his followers of that fact, saying, "My Father is greater than I."

When he appeared to his disciples after the Resurrection, he said: "As my Father hath sent me, even so send I you." (John 20:21.)

And he added: "Behold, I send the promise of my Father upon you: but tarry ye in the city of Jerusalem until ye be endued with power from on high." (Luke 24:49.)

"Go ye therefore," he said, "and teach all nations, baptizing them in the name of the Father, and of the Son, and of the Holy Ghost." (Matthew 28:19.)

It is a notable fact that he commanded that we be baptized in the name of the Father, as well as in his own name, and that of the Holy Ghost.

In the Book of Mormon, the teachings in Third Nephi are replete with similar references to the relationship between the Savior and the Father, and so he taught the Nephites, "Let your light so shine before this people, that they may see your good works and glorify your Father who is in heaven." (3 Nephi 12:16.)

He instructed them further that he had given them the "commandments of my Father. . . . therefore, come unto me, and be ye saved" (3 Nephi 12:18-20), here again indicating that we must do the will of the Father, but through the Beloved Son, our Savior, the only name under heaven whereby we may come unto the Father and be saved.

The Father stood at the head of the work, and this Jesus acknowledged.

In these latter days, the influence of the Father has been constant, either through his own appearance or through the word of his Beloved Son.

The Father was in the Sacred Grove with Jesus as Joseph Smith was given his boyhood vision. It was the Father who spoke first; it was the Father who referred Joseph to Jesus.

As the Savior recognized and deferred to the Father in his position of priority, so the Father acknowledged the Son in his capacity. Neither went beyond his own station. Each recognized the position of the other.

To Joseph Smith the Father said, referring to the Savior at his side, "This is My Beloved Son. Hear Him!" (Joseph Smith 2:17.)

It was like the occasion of the Savior's baptism, when once more the Father spoke: "Thou art my Beloved Son; in thee I am well pleased." (Luke 3:22.)

Again on the mount of Transfiguration, the Father acknowledged and honored his Beloved Son by saying to the disciples: "This is my beloved Son, in whom I am well pleased; hear ye him." (Matthew 17:5.)

When the Savior began giving revelations to the Prophet Joseph Smith, the eternal pattern was repeated. Jesus always acknowledged his Father, and gave full honor to him.

The early brethren in our Church were urged to pray to the Father, in the name of Christ. (See D&C 18:18, 40.) That name was given *of* the Father for our salvation. (See D&C 18:23.)

Jesus said he came into the world by the will of the Father and that he accomplished all things according to the will of the Father. (See D&C 19:2.) Jesus glorified the Father. (See D&C 76:43.) In the end he will deliver up the kingdom to the Father. (See D&C 76:107.) He says that the many mansions of heaven are in "my Father's house." (See D&C 81:6; 98:18.)

In the covenant of the priesthood the Father is the central figure. (See D&C 84:37-40.)

As we endeavor to be saved in the kingdom "of my Father," we are instructed that no man may come unto the Father but through Jesus Christ, the Savior. (See Acts 4:12; D&C 132:12.)

Many other references might be mentioned here, but these will suffice. The Savior constantly had an eye single to God, his Father, and we are commanded to follow his example.

And why? Because, as Paul said, we are the offspring of God (Acts 17:29), and Jesus commanded that we shall become like our Heavenly Father.

As the family of God, should we not become like him? It is not only expected of us, but it is commanded, for the Savior said, in pointing the way: "Be ye therefore perfect, even as your Father which is in heaven is perfect." (Matthew 5:48.)

And so he teaches:

"Seek ye first the kingdom of God and his righteousness." (Matthew 6:33.)

What a concentration of effort that will require!

Chapter Seventeen

Heirs of God

The fatherhood of God truly means that we are his children, his literal offspring.

Paul made this abundantly clear in his teachings. Not only did he tell the Greeks on Mars' Hill that we are the offspring of God (see Acts 17), but he taught it also to both the Romans and the Hebrews.

No one accepting the four gospels can doubt that we are indeed the children of our Heavenly Father. References to God as our Father are frequent in the teachings of Jesus.

Paul made clear that we are dual beings, that we are spirits clothed in bodies of flesh. With this in mind, he said to the Hebrews: "We have had fathers of our flesh which corrected us, and we gave them reverence: shall we not much rather be in subjection unto the Father of spirits and live?" (Hebrews 12:9.)

God, the Almighty, the Father of Christ, is also the Father of our spirits. We lived with him in our preexistent state; we were his family, were taught of him, and were told that eventually we would be sent to earth to receive bodies that we might continue to progress and ultimately become like him, if we follow his pattern.

The Lord referred to this in the book of Job, where we read:

"Where wast thou when I laid the foundations of the earth? declare, if thou hast understanding.

"Who hath laid the measures thereof, if thou knowest? or who hath stretched the line upon it?

"Whereupon are the foundations thereof fastened? or who laid the corner stone thereof;

"When the morning stars sang together, and all the sons of God shouted for joy?" (Job 38:4-7.)

President Joseph F. Smith taught that Jesus, in his pre-existent life, was a spirit child of God, even as we were also:

"Jesus Christ is not the Father of the spirits who have taken or yet shall take bodies upon this earth. . . . He is the Son, as they are sons and daughters of Elohim. So far as the stages of eternal progression and attainment have been made known through divine revelation, we are to understand that only resurrected and glorified beings can become parents of spirit offspring. Only such exalted souls have reached maturity in the appointed course of eternal life; and the spirits born to them in the eternal worlds will pass in due sequence through the several stages or estates by which glorified parents have attained exaltation." (Joseph F. Smith, *Gospel Doctrine* [Salt Lake City: Deseret Book Company, 1977], pp. 69-70: hereafter cited as *Gospel Doctrine.*)

The First Presidency in the days of President Joseph F. Smith wrote the following as a reply to an inquiry on this subject:

"Dear Sister: The First Presidency have nothing to advance concerning pre-existing states but that which is contained in the revelations to the Church. The written standards of scripture show that all people who come to this earth and are born in mortality had a pre-existent, spiritual personality as the sons or daughters of the Eternal Father. (See Pearl of Great Price, Chap. 3, verses 5-7.)

"Jesus Christ was the Firstborn. A spirit born of God is an immortal being. When the body dies the spirit does not die. In the resurrected state the body will be immortal as well as the spirit. Speculations as to the career of Adam before he came to the earth are of no real value. We learn by revelation that he was Michael, the Archangel, and that he stands at the head of his posterity on earth (Doctrine and Covenants, Sec. 107:53-56.) Dogmatic assertions do not take the place of revelation, and we should be satisfied with that which is accepted as doctrine, and not discuss matters that, after all disputes, are merely matters of theory.

Your brethren,

Joseph F. Smith,

Anthon H. Lund,

Charles W. Penrose,

First Presidency."

(— *Young Woman's Journal*, Vol. 23, pp. 162, 163, 1912.)

President Smith also said:

"Among the spirit children of Elohim, the first-born was and is Jehovah, or Jesus Christ, to whom all others are juniors." (*Gospel Doctrine*, p. 70.)

It is this Father of spirits — Elohim, the Almighty God — who is referred to by Paul as the Father of spirits to whom we should give reverence. (See Hebrews 12:9.)

But Paul taught something further. He said to the Romans:

"The Spirit itself beareth witness with our spirit, that we are the children of God:

"And if children, then heirs; heirs of God, and joint-heirs with Christ; if it so be that we suffer with him, that we may be also glorified together." (Romans 8:16-17.)

This puts further light upon the Savior's command to be perfect as our Father in heaven. (See Matthew 5:48.)

Isn't it natural that children here should become like their earthly parents? Isn't it just as natural that we should become like our heavenly Parent? Not only is it natural, not only is it possible, but it is commanded of us!

"Be ye therefore perfect, even as your Father which is in heaven is perfect." (Matthew 5:48.)

The whole plan of God is embodied in those few words. We are his children. We can become like him, and as the family of God we may go on to perfection in the eternities by

obeying the gospel of Jesus Christ, the Lord. There is no end
to existence. There is no end to our possibilities. We can be
like the infinite God.

As William W. Phelps expressed it:

> The works of God continue,
> And worlds and lives abound,
> Improvement and progression
> Have one eternal round.
>
> There is no end to matter;
> There is no end to space;
> There is no end to spirit,
> There is no end to race.

And we are his race — the literal offspring of God.

When we received the oath and covenant of the priesthood, the Lord said:

"And also all they who receive this priesthood receive
me, saith the Lord;

"For he that receiveth my servants receiveth me;

"And he that receiveth me receiveth my Father;

"And he that receiveth my Father receiveth my Father's
kingdom; therefore all that my Father hath shall be given unto
him.

"And this is according to the oath and covenant which
belongeth to the priesthood.

"Therefore, all those who receive the priesthood, receive
this oath and covenant of my Father, which he cannot break,
neither can it be moved.

"But whoso breaketh this covenant after he hath received
it, and altogether turneth therefrom, shall not have forgiveness of sins in this world nor in the world to come." (D&C
84:35-41.)

Discoursing on this subject, President Joseph F. Smith
said:

"We will progress and develop and grow in wisdom and
understanding, but our identity can never change. We did not
spring from spawn. Our spirits existed from the beginning,
have existed always, and will continue forever.

"We did not pass through the ordeals of embodiment in

lesser animals in order to reach the perfection to which we have attained in manhood and womanhood, in the image and likeness of God.

"God was and is our Father, and [we,] his [spirit] children were begotten [here] in the flesh . . . [in] his own image and likeness, male and female." (*Gospel Doctrine*, p. 25.)

Jehovah, who is Jesus Christ, the Firstborn to God in the spirit, followed the heavenly instructions, and developed to the point where he reached divinity before he was born in the flesh.

After his atonement on earth, he was given "all power both in heaven and in earth." Even before his suffering, but on the eve of it, he told the apostles: "All things that the Father hath are mine." (John 16:15.) He indeed inherited "all that my Father hath."

But within our station, we, too, may achieve perfection in eternity, for we also are "heirs of God, and joint-heirs with Christ."

By righteous living we may truly receive such an inheritance.

But let us keep in mind that although the gospel speaks much of the future eternity, it is also a gospel for here and now.

Man *is* that he may have joy, both here and hereafter. The greater the joy of this life, the greater the preparation for the next one.

Let us obtain the greatest possible joy now — in mortality. See what the gospel did for the Nephites when they kept the commandments. It is described in 4 Nephi.

Chapter Eighteen

The Vast Creations

Have you ever looked into the sky on a clear, starry night, and wondered what the Milky Way is — that band of light that extends from horizon to horizon?

It is the vast galaxy to which we, in our solar system, belong. It is like a great wheel in the sky made up of 100 billion planetary systems like our own, and it whirls around a common center, like a wheel.

Since our solar system is located on the edge of the Milky Way, when we look at it we are gazing inward from the "rim" of the "wheel." That is why the galaxy has the appearance of a light streak across the sky. As we look into the depth of the wheel from the rim we see many stars apparently on a level with each other, just as we see the spokes of a wheel from its rim. Their combined light makes this luminous band across the heavens.

How big is this Milky Way, with its 100 billion planetary systems?

Compare its size with that of our own solar system. Our planets move around the sun, which is the center of our system. From the sun to the planet Pluto, the outermost body in this system, is a distance of 3,666 million miles. The entire diameter of our solar system then is slightly less that 8,000 million miles.

Or, look at it this way: Light, traveling at the rate of 186,000 miles per second, requires eight minutes to go from the sun to our earth. That is a distance of roughly 93 million miles. It takes approximately ten hours for the sun's light to reach Pluto over its distance of 3,666 million miles.

That gives us some idea as to the size of our own solar system. But ours is only one of a hundred billion such planetary systems in the Milky Way.

Our Milky Way is nearly flat, with a slight bulge in the center, according to the astronomers. It whirls in space like a wheel. How fast does it go?

With any wheel, a given point on the rim moves faster than its inner parts. Since we and our solar system are on the outer edge of this spiral, we move at its highest velocity.

According to Fred Hoyle, noted British astronomer, that speed is half million miles per hour. At that rate it will require our sun and its universe 200 million years to complete one circuit around the Milky Way. So vast is our galaxy.

Our Milky Way, however, is only a small section of the heavens. It is part of a larger organization in the skies made up of nineteen such spirals as ours. And how big is this larger organization?

In order to have a more convenient method of measuring distance in the skies, the astronomers invented the term *parsec*. Traveling at the rate of 186,000 miles per second, light would require three years to travel one parsec.

The larger spiral to which our Milky Way galaxy belongs with these eighteen others in the same system is one million parsecs in diameter.

One of these eighteen other galaxies in this system is Andromeda, which, from where we are, is on the opposite side of this greater organization in the heavens. Andromeda is slightly larger than the Milky Way, and has more suns and planetary systems than ours.

As Fred Hoyle expressed it, if we wish to have some further idea of the extent of creation, we might realize that this larger system consisting of nineteen galaxies, including the Milky Way, "is just tucked away in one corner of the heavens." (Fred Hoyle, *Frontiers of Astronomy* [New York: Harper & Brothers, 1955].)

Astronomers have never found the outer edge of space. With the largest telescopes they only see a continuing expanse of millions of suns, stars, galaxies, nebulae and gases. There seems to be no end.

It was this that persuaded Rudolf Thiel to ask the questions: "Can it go on forever? Is an eternally expanding universe conceivable?" (Rudolf Thiel, *And There Was Light* [New York: Alfred A. Knopf, 1957], p. 389.)

And of course the Lord provides the answer with a positive yes.

Under divine inspiration, William W. Phelps put the answer into verse when he said:

> If you could hie to Kolob
> In the twinkling of an eye,
> And then continue onward,
> With that same speed to fly,
> Do you think that you could ever
> Through all eternity
> Find out the generation
> Where Gods began to be?
>
> Or see the grand beginning
> Where space did not extend?
> Or view the last creation
> Where Gods and matter end?
> Methinks the Spirit whispers
> "No man has found pure space"
> Nor seen the outside curtains
> Where nothing has a place.
>
> The works of God continue,
> And worlds and lives abound;
> Improvement and progression
> Have one eternal round.

There is no end to matter,
There is no end to space;
There is no end to spirit,
There is no end to race.

When the Lord gave us what we know as section 88 of the Doctrine and Covenants, he taught us a great lesson about space. Said he:

"All kingdoms have a law given;

"And there are many kingdoms; for there is no space in the which there is no kingdom; and there is no kingdom in which there is no space, either a greater or a lesser kingdom.

"And unto every kingdom is given a law; and unto every law there are certain bounds also and conditions. . . .

"And again, verily I say unto you, he hath given a law unto all things, by which they move in their times and their seasons;

"And their courses are fixed, even the courses of the heavens and the earth, which comprehend the earth and all the planets.

"And they give light to each other in their times and in their seasons, in their minutes, in their hours, in their days, in their weeks, in their months, in their years — all these are one year with God, but not with man.

"The earth rolls upon her wings, and the sun giveth his light by day, and the moon giveth her light by night, and the stars also give their light, as they roll upon their wings in their glory, in the midst of the power of God.

"Unto what shall I liken these kingdoms, that ye may understand?

"Behold, all these are kingdoms, and any man who hath seen any or the least of these hath seen God moving in his majesty and power." (D&C 88:36-38, 42-47.)

The Lord gave lessons in astronomy to various of the ancient prophets. Abraham was one of them. In the first chapter of the book of Abraham we read:

"But the records of the fathers, even the patriarchs, concerning the right of Priesthood, the Lord my God preserved in mine own hands; therefore a knowledge of the beginning of the creation, and also of the planets, and of the stars, as they were made known unto the fathers, have I kept even unto this day, and I shall endeavor to write some of these things upon this record, for the benefit of my posterity that shall come after me." (Abraham 1:31.)

We read this in the third chapter of Abraham:

"And I, Abraham, had the Urim and Thummim, which the Lord my God had given unto me, in Ur of the Chaldees;

"And I saw the stars, that they were very great, and that one of them was nearest unto the throne of God; and there were many great ones which were near unto it;

"And the Lord said unto me: These are the governing ones; and the name of the great one is Kolob, because it is near unto me, for I am the Lord thy God: I have set this one to govern all those which belong to the same order as that upon which thou standest.

"And the Lord said unto me, by the Urim and Thummim, that Kolob was after the manner of the Lord, according to its times and seasons in the revolutions thereof; that one revolution was a day unto the Lord, after his manner of reckoning, it being one thousand years according to the time appointed unto that whereon thou standest. This is the reckoning of the Lord's time, according to the reckoning of Kolob.

"And the Lord said unto me: The planet which is the lesser light, lesser than that which is to rule the day, even the night, is above or greater than that upon which thou standest in point of reckoning, for it moveth in order more slow; this is in order because it standeth above the earth upon which thou standest, therefore the reckoning of its time is not so many as to its number of days, and of months, and of years.

"And the Lord said unto me: Now Abraham, these two facts exist, behold thine eyes see it; it is given unto thee to know the times of reckoning, and the set time, yea, the set time of the earth upon which thou standest, and the set time of the greater light which is set to rule the day, and the set time of the lesser light which is set to rule the night.

"Now the set time of the lesser light is a longer time as to its reckoning than the reckoning of the time of the earth upon which thou standest.

"And where these two facts exist, there shall be another fact above them, that is, there shall be another planet whose reckoning of time shall be longer still;

"And thus there shall be the reckoning of the time of one planet above another, until thou come nigh unto Kolob, which Kolob is after the reckoning of the Lord's time; which Kolob is set nigh unto the throne of God, to govern all those planets which belong to the same order as that upon which thou standest.

"And it is given unto thee to know the set time of all the stars that are set to give light, until thou come near unto the throne of God.

"Thus, I, Abraham, talked with the Lord, face to face, as one man talketh with another; and he told me of the works which his hands had made;

"And he said unto me: My son, my son (and his hand was stretched out), behold I will show you all these. And he put his hand upon mine eyes, and I saw those things which his hands had made, which were many; and they multiplied before mine eyes, and I could not see the end thereof.

"And he said unto me: This is Shinehah, which is the sun. And he said unto me: Kokob, which is star. And he said unto me: Olea, which is the moon. And he said unto me: Kokaubeam, which signifies stars, or all the great lights, which were in the firmament of heaven.

"And it was in the night time when the Lord spake these words unto me: I will multiply thee, and thy seed after thee, like unto these; and if thou canst count the number of sands, so shall be the number of thy seed.

"And the Lord said unto me: Abraham, I show these things unto thee before ye go into Egypt, that ye may declare all these words.

"If two things exist, and there be one above the other, there shall be greater things above them; therefore Kolob is the greatest of all the Kokaubeam that thou hast seen, because it is nearest unto me." (Abraham 3:1-16.)

The Lord gave Enoch some idea of the number of his creations. The scripture reads:

"And were it possible that man could number the particles of the earth, yea, millions of earths like this, it would not be a beginning to the number of thy creations; and thy curtains are stretched out still; and yet thou art there, and thy bosom is there; and also thou art just; thou art merciful and kind forever." (Moses 7:30.)

But how did creation come about? How are these vast heavenly systems kept in their places? How do they maintain the precision which is so characteristic of them?

Sir Ambrose Fleming, noted British scientist and author of many articles and books on scientific subjects, wrote this:

"We have no scientific ground . . . for supposing that the vastly . . . complicated structure which we call the physical Universe has come into existence by a process of self-creation or accident, and without any connection with or dependence on an intelligent Thinker." (Ambrose Fleming, *The Origin of Man* [London: Marshall, Morgan & Scott, Ltd., 1935], p. 48.)

Edwin B. Frost, former director of Yerkes Observatory and a member of the faculty of Chicago University, wrote a book in which he said:

"Might we not expect that among the millions of suns we should find a great many kinds of matter representing thousands of chemical elements? We do not, however, find any such variety, and the testimony of the spectroscope is sufficient.

"The atom of hydrogen is shown to be the same throughout the universe, and it is found in every self-luminous celestial object yet observed. Similarly the atoms of the other elements do not vary from star to star. . . .

"We learn that our sun is like most distant stars, and that our earth is chemically quite the same as the sun, and finally that our own bodies are composed of the more common elements of the earth. Thus we may regard ourselves as samples of the whole universe." (Edwin B. Frost, *The Heavens Are Telling* [Chicago: American Institute of Sacred Literature, 1924], p. 19.)

This is most interesting, since God "formed man from the dust of the ground and took his spirit (that is, the man's spirit), and put it into him; and breathed into his nostrils the breath of life, and man became a living soul." (Abraham 5:7.)

It was Sir James Jeans, British astronomer, who said:

"The new knowledge compels us to revise our hasty first impressions that we had stumbled into a universe which either did not concern itself with life or was actively hostile to life.

"We discover that the universe shews evidence of a designing or controlling power that has something in common with our own individual minds." (Sir James Jeans, *The Mysterious Universe* [New York: The Macmillan Company, 1934], p. 186.)

He then describes the Creator as the Perfect Mathematician who expressed himself in processes capable of mathematical formulation.

The astronomers repeatedly speak of the precision which is so obvious in the movements of the heavenly bodies. Our recent space explorations and visits to the moon are evidence of this great fact.

The earth hurtles on its orbit around the sun at the rate of 66,000 miles per hour.

The moon is moving around the earth at a high velocity, also, and it, too, is traveling around the sun with the earth in its orbit, at this same rate of 66,000 miles per hour.

How could scientists on earth compute the formula by which men on a missile could leave our planet, fly into space and meet a fast-moving target such as the moon at a particular place and time?

Only because of the precision — the stability of the pattern — of movement of the heavenly bodies was it possible. And the trajectory could only be arrived at by the use of higher mathematics. Was not the Creator a mathematician?

Dr. Frost of Yerkes further adds:

"There is no adequate evidence known to the writer that the universe is automatic, that it has within itself the power to make laws which govern it. Mere matter cannot be imagined to be endowed with such capacity." (Frost, *The Heavens Are Telling*.)

Dr. John Cleveland Cothran, mathematician and chemist of Cornell University, says:

"Lord Kelvin, one of the world's greatest physicists, has

made the following statement: 'If you think strongly enough, you will be forced by science to believe in God.' I must declare myself in full agreement with this statement. . . .

"Matter, as an aggregate of molecules and atoms; the molecules and atoms themselves; their constituent protons, electrons, neutrons; electricity; energy itself — are all found to obey appropriate laws, not the dictates of chance. So true is this that 17 atoms of element 101 sufficed for its identification. The material universe is unquestionably one of system and order, not chaos; of laws, not chance and haphazards.

"Can any informed and reasoning intellect possibly believe that insensible and mindless matter just chanced to originate itself and all this system, then chanced to impose the system upon itself, whereafter this system just chances to remain imposed? Surely the answer is 'No!' When energy transforms into 'new' matter the transformation proceeds 'according to law' and the resulting matter obeys the same laws that apply to the matter already existing. . . .

"Now, the material realm not being able to create itself and its governing laws, the act of creation must have been performed by some non-material agent. The stupendous marvels accomplished in that act show that this agent must possess superlative intelligence, an attribute of *mind*.

"But to bring mind into action in the material realm, as, for example, in the practice of medicine and in the field of parapsychology, the exercise of *will* is required, and this can be exerted only by a *person*.

"Hence our logical and inescapable conclusion is not only that creation occurred but that it was brought about according to the plan and will of a *person* endowed with supreme intelligence and knowledge (omniscience), and the power to bring it about and keep it running according to plan (omnipotence) always and everywhere throughout the universe (omnipresence).

"That is to say, we accept unhesitatingly the fact of the existence of 'the supreme spiritual Being, God, the Creator and Director of the universe.'

"The advances that have occurred in science since Lord Kelvin's day would enable him to state more emphatically than ever: 'If you think strongly enough you will be forced by science to believe in God.' " (John Cleveland Cothran, "The Inescapable Conclusion," *The Evidence of God in an Expanding Universe,* p. 37.)

Agreeing with these scientists is Dr. Claude M. Hathaway of the University of Colorado, who was the designer of the "electric brain" (computer) for the National Advisory Committee on Aeronautics, specialist in electrical and physical measurements and measuring instruments, and designer for General Electric Company, Schenectady, New York. Says Dr. Hathaway:

"*Design requires a designer.* This most fundamental rational reason for my belief in God is one which has been greatly bolstered by my engineering experience.

"After years of work in the development and design of complicated mechanisms and electronics circuitry I have acquired a tremendous appreciation for *design* wherever I find it.

"With such a background, it is unthinkable that the inconceivably marvelous design in the world around us could be anything else than the product of a personal and infinitely intelligent Designer. Certainly, this is an old argument, but it is an argument that modern science has made more powerful than ever before. . . .

"After working on this computer for a year or two, and after facing and solving the many design problems which it presented, it is completely irrational to me to think that such a device could come into being in any other way than through the agency of an intelligent designer.

"Now, the world around us is a vast assembly of design or order, independent but interrelated, vastly more complex in every detail than my 'electronic brain.' If my computer required a designer, how much more so did that complex physio-chemical-biological machine which is my human body — which in turn is but an extremely minute part of the well-nigh infinite cosmos?

"Design, order, arrangement, call it what you will, can result from only two causes: chance or design. The more complex the order, the more remote the possibility of chance.

Placed as we are in the midst of design little short of infinite, I cannot help but believe in God." (Claude M. Hathaway, "The Great Designer," *The Evidence of God in an Expanding Universe*, pp. 144-45.)

Dr. Alfred G. Fisk of San Francisco State University wrote *The Search for Life's Meaning*. In that publication he quotes three scientists of note, as follows:

Fraser-Harris, British physiologist:

"So striking a oneness is perceived throughout the Universe, such a high degree of precision characterizes both nonliving and living matter that we seem forced to picture the Universe as the outcome of an Intelligent Purpose. Each of the sciences tells the same story — self-consistent, uniformity of plan."

Albert Einstein:

"The harmony of natural law reveals an intelligence of such superiority that, compared with it, all the systematic thinking and acting of human beings is an utterly insignificant reflection."

Sir James Jeans:

"From the intrinsic evidence of His creation, the Great Architect of the Universe now begins to appear as a pure mathematician."

Fisk then adds for himself:

"Faith . . . does not contradict the position of science. Just as the ordered structure of the universe implies a creative Intelligence, Architect, or Orderer, so a belief in the objectivity of purposiveness or teleology in the universe leads to the belief in a Purposer or Divine Agent who is the source and spring of purpose in the universe." (Alfred G. Fisk, *The Search for Life's Meaning* [New York: Fleming H. Revell Company, 1949], pp. 90, 92.)

And who was this Purposer, Divine Agent, Architect or Orderer?

Jehovah, Lord of Heaven and Earth, the Son of God — Christ, the Lord!

"All things were made by him; and without him was not anything made that was made." (John 1:3.)

It is no wonder that the late Dr. Shailer Mathews of the

University of Chicago, in his pamphlet "How Science Helps Our Faith," said:

"Our modern scientific thought is giving us a new basis for our faith in the existence of an infinite God: the very God revealed to us by Jesus Christ. It is giving us new material for our theology."

Chapter Nineteen

Christ the Creator

The Creation was planned long before our earth came into existence, and we lived with God during the planning period.

Creation was no accident. It didn't just happen. It was not the result of some spontaneous, uncontrolled and undirected explosion in space. And it didn't come from nothing, for nothing can only produce nothing. It was planned. Existing matter was organized into what we have today.

So it is that the scripture explains that God "said unto those who were with him: We will go down, for there is space there, and we will take of these materials, and we will make an earth. . . ." (Abraham 3:24.)

The scripture continues: "And they went down at the beginning, and they, that is the Gods, organized and formed the heavens and the earth." (Abraham 4:1.)

Creation was twofold. First came the spiritual, then came the physical, for all things were made spiritually before they were temporally. But planning preceded the creations, so actually there were three steps:

First it was planned, deliberately and with purpose.

Second, the spiritual phase of creation took place.

And third, the spiritual was clothed upon with mortality, and earth life as we know it resulted.

As the offspring of God (see Acts 17), we lived with him in an eternity before our present earth life. We are his children and may become heirs of God and joint heirs with Christ. (See Romans 8:16-17; Hebrews 12:9.)

"The Lord possessed me in the beginning of his way, before his works of old.

"I was set up from everlasting, from the beginning, or ever the earth was.

"When there were no depths, I was brought forth; when there were no fountains abounding with water.

"Before the mountains were settled, before the hills was I brought forth.

"While as yet he had not made the earth, nor the fields, nor the highest part of the dust of the world.

"When he prepared the heavens, I was there: when he set a compass upon the face of the depth:

"When he established the clouds above: when he strengthened the fountains of the deep:

"When he gave to the sea his decree, that the waters should not pass his commandment: when he appointed the foundations of the earth:

"Then I was by him, as one brought up with him: and I was daily his delight, rejoicing always before him." (Proverbs 8:22-30.)

Job understood this fact also, as noted above, for the Lord asked him:

"Where wast thou when I laid the foundations of the earth? declare, if thou hast understanding.

"When the morning stars sang together, and all the sons of God shouted for joy?" (Job 38:4, 7.)

In that preexistent time, before the earth was formed, plans were made for its ultimate use and occupation by the children of God. We were told that we could come to earth and enjoy mortal life. But a Savior must be chosen for us. Lucifer offered his services on a basis of compulsion and rebellion against the Almighty. He was rejected.

Lucifer, who later became Satan, had stood before the Father and said: "Behold, here am I, send me, I will be thy son, and I will redeem all mankind, that one soul shall not be lost, and surely I will do it; wherefore give me thine honor.

"But, behold, my Beloved Son, which was my Beloved and Chosen from the beginning, said unto me — Father, thy will be done, and the glory be thine forever.

"Wherefore, because that Satan rebelled against me, and sought to destroy the agency of man, which I, the Lord God, had given him, and also, that I should give unto him mine own power; by the power of mine Only Begotten, I caused that he should be cast down;

"And he became Satan, yea, even the devil, the father of all lies, to deceive and to blind men, and to lead them captive at his will, even as many as would not hearken unto my voice." (Moses 4:1-4.)

There in that primeval council the planning was done, and there the Savior was chosen. He was Jehovah, as he was known then, Jesus of Nazareth, as he was called in mortality.

The Lord spoke further to Moses, telling about the Creation, and that Jehovah participated:

"Behold, I reveal unto you concerning this heaven, and this earth; write the words which I speak. I am the Beginning and the End, the Almighty God; by mine Only Begotten I created these things; yea, in the beginning I created the heaven, and the earth upon which thou standest." (Moses 2:1.)

Note these words: "By mine Only Begotten I created these things."

The Lord explains further, as the scripture reads:

"And it came to pass that Moses called upon God, saying: Tell me, I pray thee, why these things are so, and by what thou madest them?

"And behold, the glory of the Lord was upon Moses, so that Moses stood in the presence of God, and talked with him face to face. And the Lord God said unto Moses: For mine own purpose have I made these things. Here is wisdom and it remaineth in me.

"And by the word of my power, have I created them,

which is mine Only Begotten Son, who is full of grace and truth.

"And worlds without number have I created; and I also created them for mine own purpose; and by the Son I created them, which is mine Only Begotten." (Moses 1:30-33.)

The scripture continues in explanation:

"But only an account of this earth, and the inhabitants thereof, give I unto you. For behold, there are many worlds that have passed away by the word of my power. And there are many that now stand, and innumerable are they unto man; but all things are numbered unto me, for they are mine and I know them.

"And it came to pass that Moses spake unto the Lord, saying: Be merciful unto thy servant, O God, and tell me concerning this earth, and the inhabitants thereof, and also the heavens, and then thy servant will be content.

"And the Lord God spake unto Moses, saying: the heavens, they are many, and they cannot be numbered unto man; but they are numbered unto me, for they are mine.

"And as one earth shall pass away, and the heavens thereof even so shall another come; and there is no end to my works, neither to my words.

"For behold, this is my work and my glory — to bring to pass the immortality and eternal life of man.

"And now, Moses, my son, I will speak unto thee concerning this earth upon which thou standest; and thou shalt write the things which I shall speak." (Moses 1:35-40.)

Paul also speaks of the Creation having been accomplished by the Almighty through the agency of Christ:

"God, who at sundry times and in divers manners spake in time past unto the fathers by the prophets,

"Hath in these last days spoken unto us by his Son, whom he hath appointed heir of all things, by whom also he made the worlds." (Hebrews 1:1-2.)

Still further word is given in section 76 of the Doctrine and Covenants, as the Lord taught the Prophet Joseph Smith this same great lesson:

"And now, after the many testimonies which have been

given of him, this is the testimony, last of all, which we give of him: That he lives!

"For we saw him, even on the right hand of God; and we heard the voice bearing record that he is the Only Begotten of the Father —

"That by him, and through him, and of him, the worlds are and were created, and the inhabitants thereof are begotten sons and daughters unto God." (D&C 76:22-24.)

When John wrote his gospel, he taught this same doctrine:

"In the beginning was the Word, and the Word was with God, and the Word was God.

"The same was in the beginning with God.

"All things were made by him; and without him was not any thing made that was made." (John 1:1-3.)

Modern translations of the Bible agree with the King James Version in all important points on this reference.

The Jerusalem Bible, with the imprimatur of the Roman Catholic Church, gives this rendering:

"In the beginning was the Word, and the Word was with God and the Word was God. He was with God in the beginning. Through him all things came to be; not one thing had its beginning but through him."

The Knox (Catholic) Version reads:

"At the beginning of time the Word already was. And God had the Word abiding with him, and the Word was God. He abode at the beginning of time with God. It was through him that all things came into being, and without him came nothing that has come to be."

Barclay's Church of Scotland rendering says:

"When the world had its beginning, the Word was already there; and the Word was with God and the Word was God. He was the agent through whom all things were made, and there is not a single thing which exists in this world which came into being without him."

The Goodspeed American translation reads:

"In the beginning the Word existed. The Word was with God and the Word was divine. It was he that was with God in the beginning. Everything came into existence through him, and apart from him nothing came to be."

The New English Bible on this particular point says: "The Word was with God at the beginning and through him all things came to be; no single thing was created without him."

The Authentic New Testament has recorded it:

"In the beginning was the Word and the Word was with God, so the Word was divine. He was in the beginning with God. By him everything had being."

The New World translation reads:

"In the beginning the Word was, and the Word was with God, and the Word was A GOD; this one was in the beginning with God. All things came into existence through him and apart from him not even one thing came into existence."

And so we might go on. All of these Bible texts confirm the King James translation — and agree with modern scripture — in saying that God brought about creation by the agency of his Son. In other words, creation was accomplished by Jesus Christ, the Savior, the Jehovah of the preexistent world, with Jesus laboring under the direction of his Father.

But the Creation was twofold, as we have said: first, spiritual; second, temporal.

Abraham's record is interesting as it describes the Creation, portraying again the fact that the Son of God, under the direction of his Father, created all things.

Says the scripture:

"And then the Lord said: Let us go down. And they went down at the beginning, and they, that is the Gods, organized and formed the heavens and the earth.

"And the earth, after it was formed, was empty and desolate, because they had not formed anything but the earth; and darkness reigned upon the face of the deep, and the Spirit of the Gods was brooding upon the face of the waters.

"And they (the Gods) said: Let there be light; and there was light.

"And they (the Gods) comprehended the light, for it was bright; and they divided the light, or caused it to be divided, from the darkness." (Abraham 4:1-4.)

What Gods?

All the way through the story of creation Abraham speaks in terms of "the Gods said," or "the Gods organized the earth" or "the Gods organized the two great lights," and "the Gods set them in the heavens to give light upon the earth," etc.

When he speaks of the creation of man, Abraham writes: "And the Gods formed man from the dust of the ground." (Abraham 5:7.)

But what Gods?

Moses answers and makes this abundantly clear:

"And I, God, said unto mine Only Begotten, which was with me from the beginning: Let us make man in our image, after our likeness. . . ." (Moses 2:26.)

It is interesting that after the Fall, we have a similar reference, clearly showing the Father and the Son working together in the Creation.

"And I, the Lord God, said unto mine Only Begotten: Behold, the man is become as one of us to know good and evil." (Moses 4:28.)

Since the King James Bible uses this plural expression with regard both to the creation and the fall of man, confusion has resulted among many. Genesis reads: "And God said, Let us make man in our image." (Genesis 1:26.)

With respect to the Fall, Genesis says: "And the Lord God said, Behold, the man is become as one of us." (Genesis 3:22.)

And when Satan tempted Adam and Eve, he said: "Ye shall be as gods, knowing good and evil." (Genesis 3:5.)

What gods?

Why, those Gods who worked together in making the earth — the Father and the Son.

Now let us note what the Lord said to Moses concerning the fact that all things were made spiritually first, followed later by the temporal creation:

"And now, behold, I say unto you, that these are the generations of the heaven and of the earth, when they were created, in the day that I, the Lord God, made the heaven and the earth;

"And every plant of the field before it was in the earth,

and every herb of the field before it grew. For I, the Lord God, created all things, of which I have spoken, spiritually, before they were naturally upon the face of the earth. For I, the Lord God, had not caused it to rain upon the face of the earth. And I, the Lord God, had created all the children of men; and not yet a man to till the ground; for in heaven created I them; and there was not yet flesh upon the earth, neither in the water, neither in the air." (Moses 3:4-5.)

Compare that with Genesis 2:4-5. Note that the Bible also says that he created "every plant of the field before it was in the earth, and every herb of the field before it grew."

The dual nature of creation, first spiritual and then temporal, is referred to also in section 77 of the Doctrine and Covenants when the Lord replied to a question from Joseph Smith concerning the book of Revelation. The scripture reads:

"Q. What are we to understand by the four beasts, spoken of in the same verse?

"A. They are figurative expressions, used by the Revelator, John, in describing heaven, the paradise of God, the happiness of man, and of beasts, and of creeping things, and of the fowls of the air; that which is spiritual being in the likeness of that which is temporal; and that which is temporal in the likeness of that which is spiritual; the spirit of man in the likeness of his person, as also the spirit of the beast, and every other creature which God has created." (D&C 77:2.)

It is abundantly shown here that even the beasts and the creeping things were made in the spirit, after which mortal bodies were provided for all, "that which is spiritual being in the likeness of that which is temporal; and that which is temporal in the likeness of that which is spiritual; the spirit of man in the likeness of his person, as also the spirit of the beast, and every other creature which God has created."

Isn't it comforting to know that an intelligent process was followed in placing life upon the earth? Isn't it reasonable that God would provide the eternal spirit first, and that then he would clothe it with temporal mortality "tailored" to fit the spirit, when the earth was prepared for it; and that the species were determined in the spirit form before the earth was made and that life then proceeded in an orderly manner, each form of life reproducing after its own kind and not in some haphazard fashion jumping from species to species?

The first chapter of Genesis makes it clear that each form of life would have within itself the seed to reproduce itself — but after its own kind! The scripture says specifically that life would have the seed "in itself" to do so. (See Genesis 1:11-12.)

It is no wonder then that President Joseph F. Smith taught:

"We did not spring from spawn. Our spirits existed from the beginning, have existed always and will continue forever.

"We did not pass through the ordeals of embodiment in the lesser animals in order to reach the perfection to which we have attained in manhood and womanhood, in the image and likeness of God. God was and is our Father, and his [spirit] children were begotten in the flesh . . . . [in] his own image and likeness, male and female." (*Gospel Doctrine*, p. 25.)

He taught further that we never change our identity. We were ourselves in the preexistence; we are ourselves here, and we will continue to be ourselves — without any change of identity — throughout the eternities to come. (See *Gospel Doctrine*, p. 27.)

As children of God, someday we may become like him, through the redemptive powers of the Lord Jesus Christ and by our complete obedience to his gospel.

Since he was the Creator in the beginning, giving us life in the first instance, was it not altogether appropriate that he also should give us a renewal of life through the Resurrection?

He brought about the Resurrection. Through it, all mankind will live again. He created life originally, and now he has created a renewal of life through the Resurrection.

As he himself said: "I am Jesus Christ, the Son of God. I am the life and the light of the world." (D&C 11:28.)

"I am Alpha and Omega, Christ the Lord; yea, even I am he, the beginning and the end, the Redeemer of the world." (D&C 19:1.)

Truly, "all things were made by him; and without him was not anything made that was made." (John 1:3.)

Chapter Twenty

Man a Creator

When President Joseph Fielding Smith wrote *The Progress of Man*, he expressed the thought that man is by nature a creator himself.

He states: "Since man is in very deed the offspring of God, and therefore created in His image, he must be endowed with certain characteristics inherited from his Father.

"He is ordained, by virtue of his birthright, to become an intelligent, independent being within his sphere. That this might be brought about, the great gift of free agency is granted. There could be no progression, no real existence, without this great gift."

President Smith then goes on: "Of all the animate creatures on the earth, man stands out alone as a sentient being endowed with the faculty of perception and the power to gain knowledge and wisdom through his senses.

"His mind is active," President Smith continues, "and when not submerged in the depths of evil, is progressive. He reasons, calculates, and creates. He is by nature a creator, for this gift he has inherited from God his Father."

He then notes the scientific, educational and aesthetic progress of the human race, and adds: "All of these powers are increased as he draws nearer to his Creator and Father.

When he forgets the source of all these qualifications and turns from his God, then are these blessings impaired and he sinks in ignorance and sin. Without the guidance of the Divine Presence, he becomes a slave to savagery and debased ignorance, for it is the Spirit of Truth which enlightens and sustains." (Joseph Fielding Smith, *The Progress of Man* [Salt Lake City: Deseret Book Company, 1964], pp. 14, 18, 19-20.)

But no matter how far he degenerates by sinful processes, no matter how far he sinks "into the earth earthy," he still is human. He never descends to the state of "the missing link"; he may act like an animal, but he is not an animal; he remains human — always. And each human has his own eternal personal identity, as President Joseph F. Smith said.

A man can sink into the gutter, or he may arise from the gutter, but he is always the same man. He may be John Brown the intellectual, and then John Brown the degenerate, but he is still John Brown. And when he recovers himself, and arises out of those depths, and regains his former status of a respected, intellectual citizen, through it all he continues to be John Brown.

If it were true that man has evolved from the lower forms of life, why is it not equally true that he would descend again to those lower forms when he becomes degenerate?

Why has not a bird reverted to being a fish? Why has not a squirrel or a monkey reverted to reptile forms? If the change of species could move in one direction, and rise to newer heights, why not move in the opposite direction as well? But it never has and never does. No one even makes a claim of this kind.

The species never changes. Man's degeneration is not a reversion to lower species; his genes are not altered; his change is not physical as to form and makeup, his rise or fall after all is of the mind. And animals have nothing even to resemble the mentality of humans, degenerate though some may become.

Sir Ambrose Fleming in his *Evolution or Creation?* writes:

"We can note at once certain qualities in the human species not the smallest trace of which appear in the animal species. Thus no animal has ever made any weapon or tool to help its bodily endowments. It fights with teeth and claws, horns, tusks, or hoofs, but it makes no military weapon of any kind.

"Nor has any animal made a tool — spade, rake, knife, hatchet, axe, or saw. No animal makes itself any artificial dress, hat or coat, shoes or ornament, to improve its appearance, nor does it dress or arrange the hair on its head. . . . No animal has discovered how to produce fire, or even to maintain it.

"The explorer, du Chaillu, says he has seen monkeys sitting around a dying fire left by a hunter in a forest and warming their paws, but they have not sufficient intelligence to put sticks on the fire to keep it alive.

"The animal mind or intellect is static or limited. It never progresses beyond a certain point. Domestic animals which have been in contact with man for thousands of years are no further forward intellectually than at the beginning.

"On the other hand, the human mind is extremely progressive, self-educative, and assimilative. Uncultured races of men brought in contact with more advanced races adopt quickly their achievements, customs, modes of thought, and habits, and unfortunately also their vices.

"Animals undoubtedly can communicate with each other, conveying information, but they have not developed the powers of speech or rational thought to anything even remotely approaching that in the case of man." (Ambrose Fleming, *Evolution or Creation?* [London: Marshall, Morgan & Scott, Ltd., 1934], pp. 72-73.)

When Adam was placed on earth he was told to work and to "dress" the Garden of Eden, which he did, thereby learning gardening at an early age. When he and Eve transgressed the law of God, and discovered that they were naked, they willingly wore adequate clothing, not being satisfied with the breechclout coverings which later characterized "fallen man."

They were cast out of Eden and farmed and raised flocks and herds. They learned how. Some archaeologists would have us believe that the first men did not know how to farm or raise flocks, that they didn't even know about fire. But this represents only some of their miscalculations, of which there are many.

The first people, Adam and Eve and their family — their children and grandchildren and great-grandchildren, were far from ignorant. Rather, they were intelligent and well educated, for God himself was their teacher. They learned to read and write, and so taught their descendants, who wrote books — many of them — libraries full of them — the libraries which have been found in ancient lands.

The early people were brilliant, well ordered and well mannered. They were inspired by the Holy Ghost, and some of them walked and talked with God. This was part of their education. They were schooled by divine means even in such advanced subjects as mathematics and astronomy.

Considerable evidence that they knew geometry and square root has been unearthed recently. Some knew about our mathematical term *pi* — 3.14159, and obviously used it in their calculations.

Note how the Holy Ghost and the Almighty himself taught astronomy to some of those early men, particularly Enoch, who lived long before the flood, and Abraham, who lived after it. For this information see the sixth and seventh chapters of Moses and the first to third chapters of Abraham in the Pearl of Great Price.

A significant scripture from the Pearl of Great Price is the following:

"And a book of remembrance was kept, in the which was recorded, in the language of Adam, for it was given unto as many as called upon God to write by the spirit of inspiration;

"And by them their children were taught to read and write, having a language which was pure and undefiled." (Moses 6:5-6.)

Recent archaeological discoveries have pushed back by many years the acknowledged time of educated early man as accepted by science. Whole libraries containing thousands of well-written and well-preserved volumes have been unearthed, dating back as far as 4,000 B.C. in the scientists' estimate of time.

This is a remarkable revision of previous time estimates.

During those early periods men built brick houses for their homes; they erected huge temples, constructed reservoirs and irrigation canals, and carried on international commerce over a much wider area than had been previously supposed. Such discoveries have been found in Mesopotamia, the so-called "cradle" of mankind.

In the "Sumerian cities of the late Fourth and early Third Millennia B.C. . . . ancient man accomplished some of his most impressive achievements in art and architecture, in social organization, in religious thought and practice and . . . in education and communication." (Samuel Noah Kramer and editors of Time-Life Books, "Great Ages of Man," *Cradle of Civilization* [New York: Time Incorporated, 1967], p. 33.)

Can such people be classed as ignorant cavemen but slightly removed from the ape?

In the Western Hemisphere, centuries before Christ, early Americans originated accurate calendars based on their astronomical observations which go well back into prehistory; they developed medicine and surgery, including brain operations and the proper setting of broken bones.

It is difficult for some to admit, but what is referred to as "the new knowledge" is giving us an entirely different view of early man, showing that many early peoples were in fact educated and progressive.

We further quote from *Cradle of Civilization*, for example:

"With the prosperity and expansion of southern Mesopotamia's early communities came an increase in the size and number of their farms and fields, and also in their irrigation canals and reservoirs which were essential to the agricultural economy; without them the land would have quickly reverted to barren desert in this virtually rainless region.

"But irrigation, especially in its more advanced stages, could be effectively carried out only as a community enterprise, not as an individual undertaking.

"Canals and reservoirs of considerable size had to be excavated, cleaned at regular intervals and kept constantly in repair. In addition, water rights had to be equitably distributed; boundary lines had to be carefully marked and authenticated; arguments had to be adjudicated and settled. [And we thought that was strictly Western and modern!]

"All these factors led to the gradual establishment of another feature facilitating city growth — a secular administration that began with a limited appointed personnel but ultimately evolved into a formidable bureaucracy with all the advantages and evils that this entails.

"Surprisingly, the government of the early Mesopotamian villages and towns was democratic; members of the ruling bodies were appointed not by a single omnipotent individual, as one might expect, but by an assembly made up of the community's free citizens." (Time-Life, *Cradle of Civilization*, p.34.)

Recall that this publication by Life and Time is not speaking of recent times — it is describing conditions reaching back into the fourth millennium B.C.

With the discovery of such conditions in prehistory now confirmed by the translation of cuneiform records recently found, it becomes apparent that all ancient peoples were not ignorant, animal-like cavemen.

It becomes fully obvious that there were at least two kinds of "dawn men" — cavemen in some areas, and intelligent, progressive and educated people in others.

It should be remembered, too, that present-day archaeology is working in two quite different fields: one in which it discovers that ancient man was intellectual and educated; the other wherein it seems he was of a very low grade.

Different scientists working in different fields make different deductions, and sometimes the conclusions of one set of scholars seem to argue against those of another.

But most scientists are honest men, and willingly revise their deductions when new information comes along. As Physicist Earl Chester Rex puts it:

"It is believed that science maintains a straight-line course in a chain of deductive reasoning. In reality, science may be likened to a climbing vine, ever trying to reach higher.

"The path of science is a devious, winding one. Carbon 14 dating, for example, is today being scrutinized if not revised. Thus, the path of science's direction must be continually changed, and oftentimes it is necessary to go back and take a different path." (Earl Chester Rex, "The Universe Under Central Control," *The Evidence of God in an Expanding Universe*, pp. 178-79.)

This should confirm in our minds the importance of holding to truth given us by revelation, and not allowing it to be overturned in our minds by an ever-changing science which is willing to revise its thinking every time new discoveries are made. Revelation doesn't have to change its mind. And revelation has much to say about early man and the dawn of life upon this planet.

Remember that all men were intelligent to begin with as God began peopling the earth through Adam and Eve. But we must recall also that the devil came among Adam's descendants, told them to "believe it not," and that many followed Lucifer.

The devil is the power of darkness, and he brought darkness into the minds of his victims. As they apostatized from the truth taught by Adam and other prophets, many regressed, became vicious, some almost animal-like. Many did go into caves and sought their food by hunting. They did not farm. They became nomads, savage and warlike. It was all a part of the regression which befell them as they apostatized from God, the sins of the parents falling upon the children, who grew up in ignorance and laziness.

Think of what happened in the so-called Dark Ages following the early Christian Era, when another apostasy descended upon the people. Consider the types of torture and despotism that prevailed in medieval Europe! Could anything be more savage than some of the atrocities perpetrated upon soldiers and civilians alike? Without the gospel do people not regress?

Lest we tend to discount these matters, it would be well to remember that in our present "enlightened age" we have our own intelligent populace, but at this very time also there are admittedly people still living on the ancient caveman level.

Go to the inner valleys of the Amazon and find them

there. Go to Paraguay and see the natives whom that government brings in from the jungles, putting them into compounds in an effort to civilize them, people who snarl, fight and eat like animals. Visit the aborigines of Australia, or those who were found recently in the Philippines; study the Hottentots, or others still extant in the present world.

Since we have these extreme opposites living on earth today, is it any wonder that similar opposites developed in 4,000 B.C.?

This condition is confirmed by Matthew W. Stirling, member of the committee for research and exploration of the National Geographic Society.

Writing a foreword for *Discovering Man's Past in the Americas*, Stirling says:

"Archaeology is, of course, the backward projection of the human story through interpretation of the material remains of past cultures. One of the remarkable things about this story is the unevenness of man's advance.

"While high civilizations developed and fell at widely scattered points, *other large segments of humanity continued to exist at primitive levels*. The anthropologists would like to know why. . . .

"The wide variation in cultural levels is made clear in descriptions of the simple hunting and gathering groups that existed throughout both [American] continents, the semi-civilized peoples of the southeastern and southwestern United States, up to the high civilizations of Middle America and western South America." (George E. Stuart and Gene S. Stuart, *Discovering Man's Past in the Americas* [Washington, D.C.: National Geographic Society, 1969], p. 5. Italics added.)

Referring to these higher cultures, many writers, including the above-mentioned Mr. and Mrs. Stuart, declare that the Meso-American culture rivaled and in some instances outstripped conditions existing in Europe at the same time.

The advanced cultures of any period, ancient or modern, are not to be judged by the evidences of primitive life found to have existed simultaneously.

We would not relish today's Western civilization being judged by the present-day aborigines. Then why should we be inclined to class all early peoples as cavemen? After all, it appears, the ancients weren't so different.

An interesting thing about "cavemen" is that even in our day, in their present state of regression, they at least retain the instinct to worship the God from whom, through the apostasy of their ancestors, they have departed, and whose nature now is unknown to them.

Schmidt's *The Origin and Growth of Religion* says that among the least civilized of mankind, and underlying their superstitious belief in polytheism, is a firm concept of one "First Father" or Great God or Great Spirit who is the Supreme Being.

He refers to the pygmies of Africa in this respect, and to the debased natives of Tierra del Fuego; to the aborigines of Australia, the Hottentots and other regressive peoples. Based on these observations, he concludes that it is innate in man to worship, and that the original faith of human beings was monotheism, not superstitious polytheism. (See pp. 61-72.)

Creative man has achieved almost superhuman levels. Think of the technology required to send men to the moon. Consider what was required to send missiles to circle Mars and Venus, and even to fly past Jupiter.

Think of man's ability to trace those missiles in space, to determine their distant courses, and to make alterations as necessary even at those distances. And think, too, of what inventive genius went into the process by which these unmanned missiles can photograph planets millions of miles away, and send back to earth pictures which may be printed in magazines and newspapers and shown on television screens.

The medical advance of human beings is amazing. But this has not been confined to modern doctors and researchers. The ancient Mayans and Incas in America set broken bones and performed surgery, including brain operations. So did the Chinese, thousands of years ago.

The engineering that went into the pyramids of both Egypt and Mexico (now believed much older than at first thought) required inventive powers only grudgingly credited to "early man." Noah built a ship to withstand the flood nearly five thousand years ago, and four thousand years ago the brother of Jared built eight submarines, and lighted and air-conditioned them for their long journey across and under the sea.

This creative genius of man came as a blessing from God. The Holy Spirit enlightens the human mind and stimulates development of needful things. It has always been so, even to some extent among the regressed races which we now think of as Stone-Age men who were dwellers in caves and crevices. (See Joel 2:28 and D&C 88.)

Man is creative. He was intended to be, because his Father was the Divine Creator!

Chapter Twenty-one

Christ the Savior

The angel Gabriel was sent from God "unto a city of Galilee, named Nazareth, to a virgin espoused to a man whose name was Joseph, of the house of David; and the virgin's name was Mary.

"And the angel came in unto her, and said, Hail, thou that art highly favoured, the Lord is with thee: blessed art thou among women.

"And when she saw him, she was troubled at his saying, and cast in her mind what manner of salutation this should be.

"And the angel said unto her, Fear not, Mary: for thou hast found favour with God.

"And, behold, thou shalt conceive in thy womb, and bring forth a son, and shalt call his name Jesus.

"He shall be great, and shall be called the Son of the Highest: and the Lord God shall give unto him the throne of his father David." (Luke 1:26-32.)

The angel further said, "That holy thing which shall be born of thee shall be called the Son of God." (Luke 1:35.)

With these words Luke describes this great event in the first chapter of his book.

As Matthew records the angelic message, he makes it known that the name of the Babe was given from heaven. He wrote, as the angel said, "Thou shalt call his name Jesus: for he shall save his people from their sins." (Matthew 1:21.)

The scripture also indicates that the holy child should be called Emmanuel, "which being interpreted is, God with us." (Matthew 1:23.)

Christ had reached divinity in his preexistent life. Hence it was altogether appropriate that when he was born one of his names should be Emmanuel, God with us, for indeed he was divine, and he now "was made flesh and dwelt among us." (John 1:14.)

But his name Jesus was equally expressive, for "he shall save his people from their sins." (Matthew 1:21.) Thereby it was indicated that he was the Savior now born in the flesh.

Having been chosen for this mission before the world was, and having created this earth as his footstool, he came here to do the will of the Father (John 5:30), who described him as "my Beloved and Chosen from the beginning" (Moses 4:2).

Of necessity the Redeemer had to be divine. No mortal could possibly take upon himself the suffering for the sins of all mankind. An infinite sacrifice was required for an infinite number of transgressions and transgressors and only Deity is infinite.

Jesus was the qualified One. He was the Firstborn, and in his preexistence had reached his divinity. As Deity he had created this earth and all the other worlds, which work itself was of infinite proportions.

He now was prepared for his next infinite assignment, the redemption of all mankind.

Two enemies were to be overcome — death and sin. Human beings must be saved from both. Only Divinity could overcome death, and only Deity could bring about the Atonement. Man could not do either.

Conquering death seems, on the surface (and be it remembered that we see only through a glass darkly), to be the less exacting of these two responsibilities which were placed upon the Savior. However, we do not know the processes of the Resurrection, nor do we know anything about the cost to bring it about.

But when the scripture speaks of the infinite suffering of the Savior, it seems to refer to his payment for the sins of man. In Gethsemane and on the cross he paid the price for the sins of all. And how great was his suffering!

He himself described it to the Prophet Joseph Smith, saying, "Which suffering caused myself, even God, the greatest of all, to tremble because of pain, and to bleed at every pore, and to suffer both body and spirit — and would that I might not drink the bitter cup, and shrink." (D&C 19:18.)

The Resurrection was glorious. It was joyful. It was also physical and real. Jesus demonstrated this as he invited his disciples to "behold my hands and my feet, that it is I myself: handle me, and see; for a spirit hath not flesh and bones, as ye see me have." (Luke 24:39.)

Though it was difficult because they had never understood the Resurrection, the disciples finally were convinced that indeed the Lord had come forth from the grave, literally and physically, and that he was now free from death. He ate before them; he blessed them; he appeared to as many as five hundred persons at once. He left no doubt in the minds of his followers concerning this great event. It had been predicted by the prophets; now it was accomplished.

His appearance to the Nephites gave further evidence of the Resurrection. Again he allowed people — twenty-five hundred of them this time — to come and "thrust their hands into his side, and . . . feel the prints of the nails in his hands and in his feet" so that they "did see with their eyes and did feel with their hands, and did know of a surety and did bear record, that it was he, of whom it was written by the prophets, that should come." (3 Nephi 11:15.)

The Resurrection will be universal, as Paul told the Corinthians, for "as in Adam all die, even so in Christ shall all be made alive." (1 Corinthians 15:22.)

But there will be different grades of glory in the Resurrection, based on "the works done in the flesh." (See 1 Corinthians 15:40-44; D&C 76; 88.)

Redemption from sin is quite another matter. Here obedience to his gospel is of paramount importance. The two are related, of course, for because of righteous living some will receive a celestial resurrection; others will receive a terrestrial or a telestial one, according to the measure of their obedience.

As John said, "all have sinned," and "whosoever committeth sin transgresseth also the law: for sin is the transgression of the law." (1 John 3:4.)

There is a punishment attached to every broken law. Had there been no redemption made, each person would be punished for his own sins and would not come out of the "prison house" until the last farthing had been paid. (See Matthew 5:26; Alma 42:15-31.)

But a redemption was made, and through it Christ paid for sin. But his redemption applies to us *only* if we obey the gospel and thus qualify to receive the benefits of his sacrifice.

Here is the great difference between the application of the Atonement to the Resurrection and to redemption from sin. All will be resurrected, whether they desire it or not. But not so with redemption from sin. Only those will receive its blessings who qualify by obedience to the gospel. The unrepentant have no claim to it.

Abinadi clearly taught this doctrine as he said:

"But remember that he that persists in his own carnal nature, and goes on in the ways of sin and rebellion against God, remaineth in his fallen state and the devil hath all power over him. Therefore, he is as though there was no redemption made, being an enemy to God; and also is the devil an enemy to God." (Mosiah 16:5.)

The Savior was very explicit on this point also as he stressed repentance. Said he:

"Behold, I, God, have suffered these things for all, *that they might not suffer if they would repent*;

"But if they would not repent, they must suffer even as I." (D&C 19:16-17. Italics added.)

This is the great point in our redemption from sin. If we

repent and serve the Lord, the redemption will apply to us. If we do not, it will be for us as though no redemption had been made. (See Mosiah 16:5.)

Unrepentant individuals will be resurrected, of course, with a lower degree of glory, but no forgiveness of sins will be granted them. It takes repentance and devout obedience to obtain forgiveness.

The Lord stressed: "If they would not repent they must suffer even as I." (D&C 19:17.) Therefore, he continued, "I command you again to repent, lest I humble you with my almighty power; and that you confess your sins, lest you suffer these punishments of which I have spoken." (D&C 19:20.)

The Lord is indeed merciful to the sinner who repents and makes the necessary adjustments. This was made clear in the Old Testament times also. Ezekiel speaks of it in this way:

"But if the wicked will turn from all his sins that he hath committed, and keep all my statutes, and do that which is lawful and right, he shall surely live, he shall not die.

"All his transgressions that he hath committed, they shall not be mentioned unto him: in his righteousness that he hath done he shall live.

"Have I any pleasure at all that the wicked should die? saith the Lord God: and not that he should return from his ways, and live?

"But when the righteous turneth away from his righteousness, and committeth iniquity, and doeth according to all the abominations that the wicked man doeth, shall he live? All his righteousness that he hath done shall not be mentioned: in his trespass that he hath trespassed, and in his sin that he hath sinned, in them shall he die." (Ezekiel 18:21-24; see also 33:12-19.)

It is interesting to note that Ezekiel says of the repentant one:

"All his transgressions that he hath committed, they shall not be mentioned unto him: in his righteousness that he hath done he shall live."

A similar thought is expressed in the Doctrine and Covenants where the Lord says:

"Behold, he who has repented of his sins, the same is forgiven, and I, the Lord, remember them no more.

"By this ye may know if a man repenteth of his sins — behold, he will confess them and forsake them." (D&C 58:42-43.)

How merciful the Lord is! If we will repent of our sins, and "keep all of my statutes" for the rest of our lives, and develop a Christlike character, we will go with Christ, and we will not be reminded of the days of our rebellion to further stir us up. We shall be forgiven and the Lord will remember our sins no more.

But the opposite is equally interesting. If a righteous man turns to iniquity, and lives the rest of his days in rebellion, and dies in his sins, none of his righteous deeds will be mentioned on the judgment day.

"All his righteousness that he hath done shall not be mentioned: in his trespass that he hath trespassed, and in his sin that he hath sinned, in them shall he die." (Ezekiel 18:24.)

Obviously, then, we are judged by the kind of character we have developed by the time of our death. If we are unrepentant, we cannot, of course, go with Christ. If we are repentant, and have been cleansed by his blood, we shall be admitted into his kingdom.

Alma explained it this way:

"But there is a law given, and a punishment affixed, and a repentance granted; which repentance mercy claimeth; otherwise, justice claimeth the creature and executeth the law, and the law inflicteth the punishment; if not so, the works of justice would be destroyed, and God would cease to be God.

"But God ceaseth not to be God, and mercy claimeth the penitent, and mercy cometh because of the atonement; and the atonement bringeth to pass the resurrection of the dead; and the resurrection of the dead bringeth back men into the presence of God; and thus they are restored into his presence, to be judged according to their works, according to the law and justice.

"For behold, justice exerciseth all his demands, and also

mercy claimeth all which is her own; and thus, none but the truly penitent are saved.

"What, do ye suppose that mercy can rob justice? I say unto you, Nay; not one whit. If so, God would cease to be God.

"And thus God bringeth about his great and eternal purposes, which were prepared from the foundation of the world. And thus cometh about the salvation and the redemption of men, and also their destruction and misery.

"Therefore, O my son, whosoever will come may come and partake of the waters of life freely; and whosoever will not come the same is not compelled to come; but in the last day it shall be restored unto him according to his deeds.

"If he has desired to do evil, and has not repented in his days, behold, evil shall be done unto him, according to the restoration of God." (Alma 42:22-28.)

The Savior is the Redeemer indeed. Of himself he said:

"I am the first and the last; I am he who liveth, I am he who was slain; I am your advocate with the Father." (D&C 110:4.)

Chapter Twenty-two

His "Other Sheep"

Jesus told the Jews that he had other sheep which were not of their fold. They did not know what he meant, and he never told them because of their unbelief.

However, he had more than just one other fold, as the Book of Mormon makes clear. We know at least about the Nephites and the lost tribes. Both were referred to by the Lord as "other sheep."

As the Savior stood among the Nephites, following his resurrection in Palestine, he said:

"Ye are my disciples; and ye are a light unto this people, who are a remnant of the house of Joseph.

"And behold, this is the land of your inheritance; and the Father hath given it unto you.

"And not at any time hath the Father given me commandment that I should tell it unto your brethren at Jerusalem.

"Neither at any time hath the Father given me commandment that I should tell unto them concerning the other tribes of the house of Israel, whom the Father hath led away out of the land.

"This much did the Father command me, that I should tell unto them:

"That other sheep I have which are not of this fold; them also I must bring, and they shall hear my voice; and there shall be one fold, and one shepherd.

"And now, because of stiffneckedness and unbelief they understood not my word; therefore I was commanded to say no more of the Father concerning this thing unto them.

"But, verily, I say unto you that the Father hath commanded me, and I tell it unto you, that ye were separated from among them because of their iniquity; therefore it is because of their iniquity that they know not of you.

"And verily, I say unto you again that the other tribes hath the Father separated from them; and it is because of their iniquity that they know not of them.

"And verily I say unto you, that ye are they of whom I said: Other sheep I have which are not of this fold; them also I must bring, and they shall hear my voice; and there shall be one fold, and one shepherd.

"And they understood me not, for they supposed it had been the Gentiles; for they understood not that the Gentiles should be converted through their preaching.

"And they understood me not that I said they shall hear my voice; and they understood me not that the Gentiles should not at any time hear my voice — that I should not manifest myself unto them save it were by the Holy Ghost.

"But behold, ye have both heard my voice, and seen me; and ye are my sheep, and ye are numbered among those whom the Father hath given me." (3 Nephi 15:12-24.)

This was spoken of and to the Americans of nearly two thousand years ago. But there were still other sheep, as the Lord himself explained:

"And verily, verily, I say unto you that I have other sheep which are not of this land, neither of the land of Jerusalem, neither in any parts of that land round about whither I have been to minister.

"For they of whom I speak are they who have not as yet heard my voice; neither have I at any time manifested myself unto them.

"But I have received a commandment of the Father that I shall go unto them, and that they shall hear my voice, and shall be numbered among my sheep, that there may be one fold and one shepherd; therefore I go to show myself unto them." (3 Nephi 16:1-3.)

The Prophet Joseph in his day said that John the Revelator was at that time among the lost tribes, preparing them for their glorious return, for they will be brought again to their homeland and will become part of the "one fold" with the "one shepherd."

The Savior explained further:

"And they who are in the north countries shall come in remembrance before the Lord; and their prophets shall hear his voice, and shall no longer stay themselves; and they shall smite the rocks, and the ice shall flow down at their presence.

"And an highway shall be cast up in the midst of the great deep.

"Their enemies shall become a prey unto them,

"And in the barren deserts there shall come forth pools of living water; and the parched ground shall no longer be a thirsty land.

"And they shall bring forth their rich treasures unto the children of Ephraim, my servants.

"And the boundaries of the everlasting hills shall tremble at their presence.

"And there shall they fall down and be crowned with glory, even in Zion, by the hands of the servants of the Lord, even the children of Ephraim.

"And they shall be filled with songs of everlasting joy.

"Behold, this is the blessing of the everlasting God upon the tribes of Israel, and the richer blessing upon the head of Ephraim and his fellows." (D&C 133:26-34.)

It is obvious that the ministry of Christ in "the meridian of time" was certainly not confined to Palestine, nor even to America. He went to his "other sheep" wherever they were and ministered to them. And the other sheep recorded these visits. They made scriptures of their own, as did the Nephites and the Jews. And so we have this:

"Know ye not that there are more nations than one? Know ye not that I, the Lord your God, have created all men, and that I remember those who are upon the isles of the sea;

and that I rule in the heavens above and in the earth beneath; and I bring forth my word unto the children of men, yea, even upon all the nations of the earth?

"Wherefore murmur ye, because that ye shall receive more of my word? Know ye not that the testimony of two nations is a witness unto you that I am God, that I remember one nation like unto another? Wherefore, I speak the same words unto one nation like unto another. And when the two nations shall run together the testimony of the two nations shall run together also.

"And I do this that I may prove unto many that I am the same yesterday, today, and forever; and that I speak forth my words according to mine own pleasure. And because that I have spoken one word ye need not suppose that I cannot speak another; for my work is not yet finished; neither shall it be until the end of man, neither from that time henceforth and forever.

"Wherefore, because that ye have a Bible ye need not suppose that it contains all my words; neither need ye suppose that I have not caused more to be written.

"For I command all men, both in the east and in the west, and in the north, and in the south, and in the islands of the sea, that they shall write the words which I speak unto them; for out of the books which shall be written I will judge the world, every man according to their works according to that which is written.

"For behold, I shall speak unto the Jews and they shall write it; and I shall also speak unto the Nephites and they shall write it; and I shall also speak unto the other tribes of the house of Israel, which I have led away, and they shall write it; and I shall also speak unto all nations of the earth and they shall write it.

"And it shall come to pass that the Jews shall have the words of the Nephites, and the Nephites shall have the words of the Jews; and the Nephites and the Jews shall have the words of the lost tribes of Israel; and the lost tribes of Israel shall have the words of the Nephites and the Jews.

"And it shall come to pass that my people, which are of the house of Israel, shall be gathered home unto the lands of their possessions; and my word also shall be gathered in one. And I will show unto them that fight against my word and against my people, who are of the house of Israel, that I am God, and that I covenanted with Abraham that I would remember his seed forever." (2 Nephi 29:7-14.)

Jesus is the Redeemer of all who will believe, both of the house of Israel and of the gentiles. He is no respecter of persons, but only those may receive his blessings who have broken hearts and contrite spirits, and come to him "as a little child."

It is not known where in America he appeared to the Nephites. The scripture says that it was in the land Bountiful, but the Book of Mormon is silent as to the geographical location of cities mentioned within its pages, at least in modern terms.

There are some who try to locate such sites in modern terms, and do so with much persuasion, but they know no more about the precise locations of these cities than they know about the location of the "other sheep" such as the lost tribes. Where are they?

What a glorious day it will be to learn of them, and to learn even further details about ancient America. What a thrilling experience it will be to study all of his word, "gathered in one."

These records will be plain and understandable, for, as Nephi himself said, "For my soul delighteth in plainness; for after this manner doth the Lord God work among the children of men. For the Lord God giveth light unto the understanding; for he speaketh unto men according to their language, unto their understanding." (2 Nephi 31:3.)

The ministry of the Savior among the Nephites was a never-to-be-forgotten experience. Among them was none of the opposition so much in evidence in Palestine. All was peaceful, all was calm. All the people believed; they wept, they prayed, they worshipped. Jesus the Christ was among them.

He had shown them the marks of the Crucifixion. Many people who saw him had heard the voice of the Father identifying him. The wicked in the land had been destroyed in the three days of terror following the Crucifixion. There were none to disturb.

All hearts were "broken"; all spirits were contrite. They were ready for the Savior; they received him with gladness, and shouted hosannahs to his holy name.

He healed their sick, raised some of their dead, blessed their children to the miraculous accompaniment of angels from heaven. He organized his Church among them, ordained twelve special disciples and gave them power to carry forward his ministry.

The people were baptized; the love of God was among them; brotherhood and sisterhood became a reality. All the people in the entire land were converted to Christ. Because of their love for each other, they had all things in common. Crime ceased; there were no more prisons; war came to an end — all because the people learned to love their neighbors as themselves.

It was a Pentecost-like experience that lasted for two centuries.

But even beyond that time, the Lord gave continued assurances to the people of ancient America pertaining to his mission. Even though wickedness subsequently came among them, even though a great falling away from the truth took place, even though the Nephites as a nation were destroyed from the face of the earth, a continual reminder was left.

Three of the twelve disciples whom Jesus had called were given power over death, and were allowed to continue to minister on the earth, and will do so even until the second coming of the Master.

Theirs is an interesting story. Before the Savior took leave of the Nephites, he "spake unto his disciples, one by one, saying unto them: What is it that ye desire of me, after that I am gone to the Father?

"And they all spake, save it were three, saying: We desire that after we have lived unto the age of man, that our ministry, wherein thou hast called us, may have an end, that we may speedily come unto thee in thy kingdom.

"And he said unto them: Blessed are ye because ye desired this thing of me; therefore, after that ye are seventy and two years old ye shall come unto me in my kingdom; and with me ye shall find rest.

"And when he had spoken unto them, he turned himself unto the three, and said unto them: What will ye that I should do unto you, when I am gone unto the Father?

"And they sorrowed in their hearts, for they durst not speak unto him the thing which they desired.

"And he said unto them: Behold, I know your thoughts, and ye have desired the thing which John, my beloved, who was with me in my ministry, before that I was lifted up by the Jews, desired of me.

"Therefore, more blessed are ye, for ye shall never taste of death; but ye shall live to behold all the doings of the Father unto the children of men, even until all things shall be fulfilled according to the will of the Father, when I shall come in my glory with the powers of heaven.

"And ye shall never endure the pains of death; but when I shall come in my glory ye shall be changed in the twinkling of an eye from mortality to immortality; and then shall ye be blessed in the kingdom of my Father.

"And again, ye shall not have pain while ye shall dwell in the flesh, neither sorrow save it be for the sins of the world; and all this will I do because of the thing which ye have desired of me, for ye have desired that ye might bring the souls of men unto me, while the world shall stand.

"And for this cause ye shall have fulness of joy; and ye shall sit down in the kingdom of my Father; yea, your joy shall be full, even as the Father hath given me fulness of joy; and ye shall be even as I am, and I am even as the Father; and the Father and I are one;

"And the Holy Ghost beareth record of the Father and me; and the Father giveth the Holy Ghost unto the children of men, because of me.

"And it came to pass that when Jesus had spoken these words, he touched every one of them with his finger save it were the three who were to tarry, and then he departed.

"And behold, the heavens were opened, and they were caught up into heaven, and saw and heard unspeakable things.

"And it was forbidden them that they should utter; neither was it given unto them power that they could utter the things which they saw and heard;

"And whether they were in the body or out of the body, they could not tell; for it did seem unto them like a transfiguration of them, that they were changed from this body of flesh into an immortal state, that they could behold the things of God.

"But it came to pass that they did again minister upon the face of the earth; nevertheless they did not minister of the things which they had heard and seen, because of the commandment which was given them in heaven.

"And now, whether they were mortal or immortal, from the day of their transfiguration, I know not;

"But this much I know, according to the record which hath been given — they did go forth upon the face of the land, and did minister unto all the people, uniting as many to the church as would believe in their preaching; baptizing them, and as many as were baptized did receive the Holy Ghost.

"And they were cast into prison by them who did not belong to the church. And the prisons could not hold them, for they were rent in twain.

"And they were cast down into the earth; but they did smite the earth with the word of God, insomuch that by his power they were delivered out of the depths of the earth; and therefore they could not dig pits sufficient to hold them.

"And thrice they were cast into a furnace and received no harm.

"And twice were they cast into a den of wild beasts; and behold they did play with the beasts as a child with a suckling lamb, and received no harm.

"And it came to pass that thus they did go forth among all the people of Nephi, and did preach the gospel of Christ unto all people upon the face of the land; and they were converted unto the Lord, and were united unto the church of Christ, and thus the people of that generation were blessed, according to the word of Jesus.

"And now I, Mormon, make an end of speaking concerning these things for a time.

"Behold, I was about to write the names of those who were never to taste of death, but the Lord forbade; therefore I write them not, for they are hid from the world.

"But behold, I have seen them, and they have ministered unto me.

"And behold they will be among the Gentiles, and the Gentiles shall know them not.

"They will also be among the Jews, and the Jews shall know them not.

"And it shall come to pass when the Lord seeth fit in his wisdom that they shall minister unto all the scattered tribes of Israel, and unto all nations, kindreds, tongues and people, and shall bring out of them unto Jesus many souls, that their desire may be fulfilled, and also because of the convincing power of God which is in them.

"And they are as the angels of God, and if they shall pray unto the Father in the name of Jesus they can show themselves unto whatsoever man it seemeth them good.

"Therefore, great and marvelous works shall be wrought by them, before the great and coming day when all people must surely stand before the judgment-seat of Christ;

"Yea even among the Gentiles shall there be a great and marvelous work wrought by them, before that judgment day....

"But behold, since I wrote, I have inquired of the Lord, and he hath made it manifest unto me that there must needs be a change wrought upon their bodies, or else it needs be that they must taste of death; ...

"And in this state they were to remain until the judgment day of Christ; and at that day they were to receive a greater change, and to be received into the kingdom of the Father to go no more out, but to dwell with God eternally in the heavens." (3 Nephi 28:1-32, 37, 40.)

Could anything but a lasting impression be left with the people following the marvelous appearance of the Savior, or after two hundred years of unexcelled peace and worship, or considering the ministry of these three men who did not taste of death?

Over the centuries these events have been recalled even

in legends and myths as years went by and memories grew dim, and man-made details filled in where facts had been obliterated.

The Christ had a worldwide ministry during "the meridian of time." It has not been forgotten, and never shall be.

Chapter Twenty-three

The Great White God

The tradition of the coming of the resurrected Christ to ancient America lives on today among the descendants of the people who saw him. It is known as the tradition of the Great White God.

After nearly two thousand years, the legends have become thin, but they still are heard in many states of the United States, in Mexico and Meso-America, South America, and in the South Seas.

Actually, they persist from Alaska to Chile and from Peru to New Zealand, for the Polynesians also trace their traditions and genealogies from their scattered islands to America, "the land of the high mountains."

New light has been thrown upon the story of the Great White God, however, and now it comes from research, not memory alone.

In the discoveries and writings of archaeologists and historians, this Being now stands out as an unassailable reality. The mystery that so long veiled the puzzling traditions of the natives is swept aside by modern research and newly found but centuries-old documents that open a widely expanded view of this Divinity and his labors in the Western Hemisphere.

There was such a God!

He did come to America, long before the time of Columbus.

He taught the ancients his true religion, raised some of their dead, healed many of their sick, taught new and more productive methods of agriculture, and established a government of equality and peace.

He came suddenly and left suddenly in a supernatural manner.

The ancients regard him as the Creator, come to earth in bodily form.

Who can doubt evidence that now mounts so high?

That he was a Christian divinity none can successfully deny.

That his teachings were akin to the Bible is now readily admitted by many.

And that he promised to return in a second coming is an acknowledged, scriptural fact, well attested by subsequent historical accounts.

The tradition of a White God in ancient America was preserved through generations of Indians from Chile to Alaska, and has been significantly persistent likewise among the Polynesians from Hawaii to New Zealand.

In their main details all such traditions agree. They differ in name and minor details from island to island and from country to country, but the overall outline remains the same — there was a Great White God. He came among their forefathers, ministered for a while, and then left again. Some say he ascended to heaven.

Of such veracity is the information now available concerning him that Paul Herrmann was induced to say in his book *Conquest by Man:*

"Carefully considered this leaves no other conclusion open than that the Light God Quetzalcoatl was a real person, that he was neither an invention of Spanish propaganda nor a legendary figment of Indian imagination." (Paul Herrmann, *Conquest by Man* [New York: Harper & Brothers, 1954], p. 172.)

This Being was known as Quetzalcoatl in parts of Mexico,

primarily in the Cholula area. He was Votan in Chiapas and Wixepechocha in Oaxaca, Gucumatz in Guatemala, Viracocha and Hyustus in Peru, Sume in Brazil, and Bochica in Colombia.

To the Peruvians he was also known as Con-tici or Illa-Tici, Tici meaning both Creator and the Light. To the Mayans he was principally known as Kukulcan.

In the Polynesian Islands he was Lono, Kana, Kane, or Kon, and sometimes Kanaloa — the Great Light or Great Brightness. He also was known as Kane-Akea, the Great Progenitor, or Tonga-roa, the god of the ocean sun.

What did he look like, this Great White God?

He was described in the native traditions as a tall, white man, bearded and with sea-blue eyes. He wore loose, flowing robes. He came from heaven, and went back to heaven.

And what did he do when he came? The traditions say that he healed the sick, gave sight to the blind, cured the lame, and raised some of the dead. He taught a better life, telling the people to do unto others as they would be done by, to love their neighbors as themselves, and to always show kindness and charity.

He seemed to be a person of great authority and unmeasured kindness. He had power to make hills into plains and plains into high mountains. He could bring fountains of water from the solid rock.

In addition to giving them rules on how to live peacefully together, he urged these ancient Americans to greater learning, and also taught them improved methods of agriculture.

One of the remarkable things about his coming was that he appeared after a period of darkness in all the land, during which the people had prayed for a return of the sun. While the darkness yet prevailed, "they suffered great hardship . . . and . . . made great prayers and vows to those they held to be their gods, imploring of them the light that had failed." As the light returned, then came this "white man, large of stature, whose air and person aroused great respect and veneration. . . . And when they saw his power, they called him the Maker of all things, their Beginner, Father of the sun."

(Victor Wolfgang von Hagen, editor, *The Incas of Pedro de Cieza de Leon,* [Norman, Oklahoma: University of Oklahoma Press, 1959], p. 27.)

This personage, as he taught his religion, also urged the people to build great temples for worship, and his followers became very devout. As he left them, he promised his second coming, which caused the natives to look for his return even as the Jews look for their promised Messiah.

This faith led to disaster, however, when the Spaniards came to America and when Captain Cook sailed to the Hawaiian Islands. But these tragedies served only to reinforce the evidence of his reality.

When the Spanish conquistadores reached South America, one of Pizarro's lieutenants strode ashore wearing his helmet and breastplate and carrying a shining musket. He made an impressive appearance.

Natives on the shore watched him in amazement. He was a white man! As Pedro de Candia strode toward them, they knelt before him and began to say "Viracocha, Viracocha." It puzzled the gallant Pedro. The natives drew nearer, surrounding him. Somewhat fearful himself, he fired his gun into the air, expecting to frighten the natives away. But they did not move. Instead they whispered, "Illa Tiki, Illa Tiki," meaning "the god of lightning."

The Indians thought he was their returning white god Viracocha, and that with his gun he controlled both thunder and lightning.

Hernando Cortez was likewise believed to be the returning White God as he came to Mexico in 1520.

Pierre Honoré's *In Quest of the White God* has these interesting paragraphs concerning the coming of Cortez and the fact that the Indians thought he was their returning Deity:

"Everywhere in the Indian states of Central and South America the legend of the White God is known, and it always ends in the same way: the White God left his people with a solemn promise that he would one day come back.

"The legend, however, was one of the main reasons for the quick downfall of the Indian states. The people had the image of the White God so firmly fixed in their minds that they immediately accepted the Spaniard as the White God who had returned.

"The Aztec priests in Mexico had worked out that their White God, who left them in the year Ce-acatl (1 Reed), would also return one day in the year Ce-acatl. In the Aztec calendar this year Ce-acatl recurs every fifty-two years. Before every such recurrence the stars and other portents were carefully observed, and each time the priests predicted whether the White God would return on the first day of the new cycle.

"By strange coincidence it was just before a new cycle started that word got around among the Aztecs of 'water houses with swan wings' cruising off their shores. Soon after the year '1 Reed' began Cortés landed on the coast of Mexico. Even the date, the day of the White God's return, tallied exactly with the one the priests had worked out from their ancient records: the White God would return in the year 1 Reed on the day '9 Wind'. The date by our reckoning was April 22nd, 1519, Maundy Thursday of that year."

This writer then concludes his chapter on the Great White God with these words:

"Enter an Indian hut in the Yucatan jungle; join the elders round their fires on the icy Bolivian plateau; talk to Indians in the jungle on the banks of the Amazon: wherever you go you will hear the legend." (Pierre Honoré, *In Quest of the White God* [New York: G. P. Putnam's Sons, 1964], pp. 17, 18.)

When the coastal natives saw that Cortez was white, a leader among his men, and that he came in a large ship with white sails, they ran hurriedly to their ruler Montezuma and announced that the Great White God had arrived.

This had a striking effect upon Montezuma. He remembered that when he was crowned as emperor, the priests of the Aztec cult reminded him: "This is not your throne; it is only lent you and will one day be returned to the One to whom it is due." (Honoré, *In Quest*, p. 66.)

Montezuma immediately made plans to greet Cortez with all the respect he owed to the White God whom his Aztec religion had taught him to expect. Precious gifts were brought to Cortez; the riches of the realm were opened to him. He was honored as a deity indeed. But his treachery soon changed that, and warfare resulted. Montezuma lost his throne and his life. But the tradition remained.

When Captain James Cook sailed into the peaceful waters of the Hawaiian Islands, he too was mistaken for the White God. The natives there, like their relatives in America, had long expected the second coming of their Great White God.

Seeing Captain Cook, a white man of high command, sailing in a large ship with great white sails such as the natives had never before seen, the naive Hawaiians received and worshiped him as their long-looked-for, golden-haired god Lono.

Remarkably, Captain Cook had landed during the Makahiki Festival, the celebration that kept alive the traditions of the White God Lono. King Kalaniopuu welcomed him and his party, and the native priests led him with high ceremony to the great stone truncated pyramid that was Lono's temple. In amazement, the redoubtable British explorer accepted their obeisance, quite willing to receive any honors they were willing to bestow upon him.

But his men were anything but angelic, and through their depredations they brought down upon the entire Cook party the wrath of the natives. In the battle that ensued, Cook lost his life.

But once again — that tradition persisted.

Not only have the oft-told stories of the White God continued through the ages, but his teachings are also still dear to the hearts of the natives.

For years, because men went to war and often were killed, women were the keepers of the traditions and genealogies. They told these stories to their children and their children's children.

One of the remarkable survivals is that recounted in Stephens's *Incidents of Travel in Central America, Chiapas, and Yucatan.* The author quotes what Fuentes, chronicler of the ancient kingdom of Guatemala and of the Toltecan Indians, said of the origin of these people.

They were Israelites, he said, released by Moses from the tyranny of the Pharaohs. After crossing the Red Sea, they became idolaters because of the influence of the local peoples; and to escape the reproofs of Moses, they strayed away. Under the leadership of a man named Tanub, they drifted from continent to continent until finally they came to a place they called the Seven Caverns, a part of the kingdom of Mexico, where they founded the city of Tula. The story recounts that from Tanub, their leader, sprang the families of the Tula and the Quiche.

Other traditions tell of four brothers who led their families from far distant lands to the east, over the oceans, to the new world where they settled and built cities.

Popol Vuh, The Sacred Book of the Ancient Quiché Maya reveals that the early Americans believed in a trinity of deities. They believed also in a Heavenly Father and a Heavenly Mother, and that the Eternal Father and his Beloved Son were the Creators of heaven and earth. The Trinity are known as Caculha-Huracan, Chipi-Caculha, and Rexa-Caulha. They were called the Heart of Heaven.

Popol Vuh also speaks of the Creation as having been accomplished by this Trinity — three deities — creators and makers of all. These early Americans, now found to have been highly cultured in many ways, and deeply religious, did not believe in any sexless, formless, phantom-like god. To them the Trinity were real persons, who had sex and personality. And there was a Mother in heaven.

These early Americans, as shown in this same volume, believed in a preexistence, and in a devil who also lived in that pre-earth life where he boasted of his brilliance and power, saying "my eyes are of silver, bright, resplendent as precious stones, as emeralds, my teeth shine like perfect stones, like the face of the sky. . . . So then I am the sun, I am the moon, for all mankind."

This evil being sought to usurp the glory of God but failed. "His only ambition was to exalt himself and to dominate," the legend says.

The manuscript from ancient Indian sources explains

that at this point "neither our first mother nor our first father had yet been created." (Adam and Eve.)

There is also the story of the woman being tempted to eat the fruit of a tree and asking, "Must I die? Shall I be lost if I pick one of this fruit?" (Delia Goetz and Sylvanus G. Morley, trans., *Popol Vuh, The Sacred Book of the Ancient Quiché Maya* [Norman, Oklahoma: University of Oklahoma Press, 1950].)

The story of the great flood (Noah's) is recounted among the early Americans and Polynesians.

Traditions in northern Mexico, principally among the Yaqui Indians, tell of the survival of a council of twelve holy men who ministered piously among the people. They also tell of a form of sacrament of the Lord's Supper, wherein the natives eat and drink sacred emblems amid signs of great sadness, in remembrance of their deity.

Religion was a vital part of the lives of these ancient Americans, as it was with the Polynesians, who, it is believed, brought their religion with them in their migrations from America. Volumes have been written about it.

Who was this Great White God?

As Jesus Christ ministered in mortality among the Jews, he spoke of another body of believers — his other sheep. (See John 10:16.) He promised to go to them and minister among them. This he did — in America.

In ancient America also prophets ministered, even as others did in Palestine, and during the same period of time.

These Western prophets wrote their sacred history, even as did their Palestinian counterparts, and in this manner another volume of scripture was prepared. Known as the Book of Mormon, it tells of God's dealings with ancient America, as the Bible relates the sacred history of the Old World.

The Book of Mormon tells the facts about the coming of the White God, an event that occurred in America following his resurrection in Palestine. Millions of people lived in America then. Some believed in the coming of Christ to their land. Others scoffed. The believers served the Lord; the scoffers followed every evil path.

When the Crucifixion took place and the earthquakes

shook Palestine, even worse quakes, tempests, and con-
flagrations swept over the Western Hemisphere. The Book of
Mormon tells the story:

"And it came to pass in the thirty and fourth year, in the
first month, on the fourth day of the month, there arose a
great storm, such an one as never had been known in all the
land.

"And there was also a great and terrible tempest; and
there was terrible thunder, insomuch that it did shake the
whole earth as if it was about to divide asunder.

"And there were exceeding sharp lightnings, such as
never had been known in all the land.

"And the city of Zarahemla did take fire." (3 Nephi
8:5-8.)

According to the account, the damage was immense.
Highways were broken up, cities were sunk, many persons
were slain, and the whole face of the land was changed — all
this in the space of about three hours.

Then, ". . . it came to pass that there was thick darkness
upon all the face of the land, insomuch that the inhabitants
thereof who had not fallen could feel the vapor of darkness."
(3 Nephi 8:20.)

After this condition, which lasted for three days, there
came a voice, ". . . and all the people did hear, and did
witness of it, saying:

"O ye people of these great cities which have fallen, who
are descendants of Jacob, yea, who are of the house of Israel,
how oft have I gathered you as a hen gathereth her chickens
under her wings, and have nourished you.

". . . how oft would I have gathered you as a hen
gathereth her chickens, and ye would not." (3 Nephi 10:3-5.)

Some days later a great multitude gathered together
about the temple in the land Bountiful, and there came a voice
three times:

"And behold, the third time they did understand the
voice which they heard; and it said unto them:

"Behold my Beloved Son, in whom I am well pleased, in
whom I have glorified my name — hear ye him.

"And it came to pass, as they understood they cast their

eyes up again towards heaven; and behold, they saw a Man descending out of heaven; and he was clothed in a white robe; and he came down and stood in the midst of them; and the eyes of the whole multitude were turned upon him, and they durst not open their mouths, even one to another, and wist not what it meant, for they thought it was an angel that had appeared unto them.

"And it came to pass that he stretched forth his hand and spake unto the people, saying:

"Behold, I am Jesus Christ, whom the prophets testified shall come into the world.

"And behold, I am the light and life of the world; and I have drunk out of that bitter cup which the Father hath given me, and have glorified the Father in taking upon me the sins of the world, in the which I have suffered the will of the Father in all things from the beginning.

"And it came to pass that when Jesus had spoken these words the whole multitude fell to the earth; for they remembered that it had been prophesied among them that Christ should show himself unto them after his ascension into heaven.

"And it came to pass that the Lord spake unto them saying:

"Arise and come forth unto me, that ye may thrust your hands into my side, and also that ye may feel the prints of the nails in my hands and in my feet, that ye may know that I am the God of Israel, and the God of the whole earth, and have been slain for the sins of the world.

"And it came to pass that the multitude went forth, and thrust their hands into his side, and did feel the prints of the nails in his hands and in his feet; and this they did do, going forth one by one until they had all gone forth, and did see with their eyes and did feel with their hands, and did know of a surety and did bear record, that it was he, of whom it was written by the prophets, that should come.

"And when they had all gone forth and had witnessed for themselves, they did cry out with one accord, saying:

"Hosanna! Blessed be the name of the Most High God!

And they did fall down at the feet of Jesus, and did worship him." (3 Nephi 11:6-17.)

In the days that followed, the same divine Visitor introduced the blessing of the bread and wine as sacrament; he called forth all their sick, afflicted, lame, blind, and dumb, and healed them; he organized an administration to teach and baptize in his name, and he counseled these leaders and the multitudes about his doctrine. And after many days, "... there came a cloud and overshadowed the multitude that they could not see Jesus.

"And while they were overshadowed he departed from them, and ascended into heaven. And the disciples saw and did bear record that he ascended again into heaven." (3 Nephi 18:38-39.)

This is the true story of the Great White God. He is Jesus the Christ, the Savior of all mankind.

Chapter Twenty-four

Fair – Pale – or White

Wherever one may go, from Alaska to Virginia, from Wyoming to Peru, from Bolivia to New Zealand, it is the same, the natives cherish the story of the miraculous appearance of a heavenly being to their ancient forefathers.

Some call him the Fair God, some the Pale God, some the White God, but the reference is the same. All speak of their ancient Divinity and the miracles he performed.

In Polynesia he is often spoken of as Wakea; in Guatemala as the Healer, in Peru the Pale One; in Brazil, Waikano; in Mexico, Quetzalcoatl.

In the Land of Panuco (state of Georgia, United States), the Indians speak of him also as the Healer, "who built a pyramid-temple with painted logs and dedicated to Our Father, the Great Spirit."

In Oklahoma the Shawnee quoted this same Healer as telling them: "Do not kill or injure your neighbor, rather love him for the Great Spirit loves him as He also loves you." This is part of their chant.

In West Virginia the Cherokees spoke of him as "The Prophet," who was "about his Father's business." He told them of his birth. He had twelve disciples.

The Pawnees say he taught them about his Father, "the Mighty Holy of the Heavens." In Mississippi it was the same.

In New York the Seneca legend says that he spoke to them of the ways of his Father and explained his religion of peace. In Michigan the Chippewas said that when he came they "covered his paths with flowers so that he would always walk on petals." His robe was long and white, and he wore golden sandals on his feet.

The Choctahs call him "Ee-me-shee," the Wind God. He told them of the coming of the white men "and when he did his eyes became sad." By the Canadian tribes the Pale God was known as the God of the Wind and the Water, "his every move bespoke his kindness."

In Wyoming the Cheyennes remember the White God who told them also of the coming of the white man.

In Washington the Yakimas called him Tacoma. He promised to return to visit them. Their chief was Seattle, known for his wisdom.

In Oregon and California, he was the Pale God Em-eeshetotl. He healed the sick, and trained twelve special disciples. He spoke eloquently and reverently of his Father.

The Arizona Hopis spoke of the Fire God and the Prophet as they referred to this same Personage who had long ago visited their forefathers. The Papagos called him E-see-Cotl who taught them: "Do not scold the little children, let them come to me."

It is possible that certain of the expressions such as "about my Father's business" and "let the children come unto me" reflect Christian teachings as they probably were given later to the Indians by the Spanish padres, but there are certain parts in these legends which could not possibly have come from the Spaniards, because they exist universally, even where no Spanish priests had come, such as the South Seas, for example, or Alaska.

One of the most interesting elements in these legends is the constant referral to "My Father," as made by this mysterious visitor. Always he spoke of him, always he was reverent in doing so, always he taught the natives to honor their Father, the Great Spirit of heaven.

An interesting book on this subject is *He Walked the Americas*, by L. Taylor Hansen, Amherst, Wisconsin: Amherst Press. Mr. Hansen spent more than thirty years studying the legends of natives of North and South America, and his work fully supports the account of the ancient visitation of a Personage with divine powers.

Thor Heyerdahl, in his remarkable book *American Indians in the Pacific*, shows how the American legends of the White God filtered across the seas among the islanders of Polynesia, and he reveals that the Maoris, in particular, regarded Him as a Personage of high intelligence, and like the brightness of the sun.

Heyerdahl most interestingly demonstrates that on some of the islands were white people, and that in fact two races — both with similar legends and traditions — lived side by side in Polynesia.

He quotes an old native Maori historian who spoke of these white people as "an Iwi Atua (a god-like race, a people of supernatural powers). In appearance some of them were very much like the Maori people of today; others resembled the Pakeha (or white) race." Their hair was red or blond, he said. (Thor Heyerdahl, *American Indians in the Pacific* [London: George Allen & Unwin, Ltd., 1952], p. 191.)

But white or dark, they carried the same tradition — the Great White God visited their forefathers many moons ago.

Chapter Twenty-five

The Second Coming

The second coming of the Savior is a certainty. He has so declared it. But it will not come without adequate warning to the people of the earth.

When God sent the flood in the days of Noah, the people were rebellious and defiant, and mocked the prophet. But the Lord gave them time to consider the message of Noah and be saved from the flood — if they would.

His second coming will have even greater warning and over a longer period of time. The warning has already begun, and will continue, for "this gospel of the kingdom shall be preached in all the world for a witness to all nations, and then shall the end come." (Matthew 24:14.)

Some have said that the coming of the Lord will have to wait until all mankind becomes righteous enough to receive him. This is a great mistake.

Others have said that his coming will be in a day of worldwide turmoil and earth-shattering destruction. Some have spoken of it as "doomsday" because its coming will spell doom for the wicked who refuse to repent.

Although it will indeed be dreadful for the unrepentant, it will, nevertheless, be a day of great rejoicing for the righteous, a day of great miracles, of the fulfilment of prophecy, and of reunion with loved ones. It will be the opening of the millennial reign of peace.

The Lord will come in the clouds of heaven and all nations "shall see him together" as the prophet said. The righteous will be caught up to meet him in the skies, and will decend with him to rule and reign on the earth for a thousand years.

Although it will be a time of destruction for the wicked, such will not be of the Lord's choosing. In his mercy, he invites all men to come unto him. "Have I any pleasure at all that the wicked should die? saith the Lord God: and not that he should return from his ways, and live?" (Ezekiel 18:23.)

But sadly enough, it will be with many now as it was with the ancients when he said:

"O Jerusalem, Jerusalem, thou that killest the prophets, and stonest them which are sent unto thee, how often would I have gathered thy children together, even as a hen gathereth her chickens under her wings, and ye would not!" (Matthew 23:37.)

"And ye would not." The stubbornness of mankind is incredible. The world is still stubborn, but nevertheless, he will send his warning before the destruction, and that warning will be the voice of the elders declaring the saving principles of his gospel, now restored in these latter days.

When the Savior gave us the preface to the Doctrine and Covenants, he gave it as a voice of warning to the world, and said:

"Hearken, O ye people of my church, saith the voice of him who dwells on high, and whose eyes are upon all men; yea, verily I say: Hearken ye people from afar; and ye that are upon the islands of the sea, listen together.

"For verily the voice of the Lord is unto all men, and there is none to escape; and there is no eye that shall not see, neither ear that shall not hear, neither heart that shall not be penetrated.

"And the rebellious shall be pierced with much sorrow; for their iniquities shall be spoken upon the housetops, and their secret acts shall be revealed.

"And the voice of warning shall be unto all people, by the mouths of my disciples, whom I have chosen in these last days.

"And they shall go forth and none shall stay them, for I the Lord have commanded them.

"Behold, this is mine authority, and the authority of my servants, and my preface unto the book of my commandments, which I have given them to publish unto you, O inhabitants of the earth.

"Wherefore, fear and tremble, O ye people, for what I the Lord have decreed in them shall be fulfilled.

"And verily I say unto you, that they who go forth, bearing these tidings unto the inhabitants of the earth, to them is power given to seal both on earth and in heaven, the unbelieving and rebellious;

"Yea, verily, to seal them up unto the day when the wrath of God shall be poured out upon the wicked without measure —

"Unto the day when the Lord shall come to recompense unto every man according to his work, and measure to every man according to the measure which he has measured to his fellow man.

"Wherefore the voice of the Lord is unto the ends of the earth, that all that will hear may hear:

"Prepare ye, prepare ye for that which is to come, for the Lord is nigh;

"And the anger of the Lord is kindled, and his sword is bathed in heaven, and it shall fall upon the inhabitants of the earth.

"And the arm of the Lord shall be revealed; and the day cometh that they who will not hear the voice of the Lord, neither the voice of his servants, neither give heed to the words of the prophets and apostles, shall be cut off from among the people;

"For they have strayed from mine ordinances, and have broken mine everlasting covenant;

"They seek not the Lord to establish his righteousness, but every man walketh in his own way, and after the image of his own God, whose image is in the likeness of the world, and whose substance is that of an idol, which waxeth old and shall perish in Babylon, even Babylon the great, which shall fall.

"Wherefore, I the Lord, knowing the calamity which should come upon the inhabitants of the earth, called upon my servant Joseph Smith, Jun., and spake unto him from heaven, and gave him commandments." (D&C 1:1-17.)

The restoration of the gospel in the latter days was a necessary prelude to Christ's coming. He is just to all mankind. He offers salvation to every one, and all who listen and serve him may have peace and protection.

Before his crucifixion, his disciples asked him about the temple in Jerusalem which he said would be destroyed, so that not one stone would rest upon the other. They asked for signs by which they could recognize the day of this tragedy. He gave them the details for which they asked.

But he gave them more. He told of the destruction to take place in the last days also, preceding his second coming. In doing so he explained that full warning would be given the world before that day should come.

As indicated in his preface, that warning would come through the restoration and preaching of the gospel, worldwide.

When the Savior gave to Joseph Smith the details of what he told his ancient disciples, he said:

"And this I have told you concerning Jerusalem; and when that day shall come, shall a remnant be scattered among all nations;

"But they shall be gathered again; but they shall remain until the times of the Gentiles be fulfilled.

"And in that day shall be heard of wars and rumors of wars, and the whole earth shall be in commotion, and men's hearts shall fail them, and they shall say that Christ delayeth his coming until the end of the earth.

"And the love of men shall wax cold, and iniquity shall abound.

"And when the times of the Gentiles is come in, a light shall break forth among them that sit in darkness, and it shall be the fulness of my gospel;

"But they receive it not; for they perceive not the light,

and they turn their hearts from me because of the precepts of men.

"And in that generation shall the times of the Gentiles be fulfilled.

"And there shall be men standing in that generation, that shall not pass until they shall see an overflowing scourge; for a desolating sickness shall cover the land.

"But my disciples shall stand in holy places, and shall not be moved; but among the wicked, men shall lift up their voices and curse God and die.

"And there shall be earthquakes also in divers places, and many desolations; yet men will harden their hearts against me, and they will take up the sword, one against another, and they will kill one another.

"And now, when I the Lord had spoken these words unto my disciples, they were troubled.

"And I said unto them: Be not troubled, for, when all these things shall come to pass, ye may know that the promises which have been made unto you shall be fulfilled.

"And when the light shall begin to break forth, it shall be with them like unto a parable which I will show you —

"Ye look and behold the fig trees, and ye see them with your eyes, and ye say when they begin to shoot forth, and their leaves are yet tender, that summer is now nigh at hand;

"Even so it shall be in that day when they shall see all these things, then shall they know that the hour is nigh.

"And it shall come to pass that he that feareth me shall be looking forth for the great day of the Lord to come, even for the signs of the coming of the Son of Man.

"And they shall see signs and wonders, for they shall be shown forth in the heavens above, and in the earth beneath.

"And they shall behold blood, and fire, and vapors of smoke.

"And before the day of the Lord shall come, the sun shall be darkened, and the moon be turned into blood, and the stars fall from heaven." (D&C 45:24-42.)

When Joseph Smith revised Matthew 24 as we have it in the Pearl of Great Price, he wrote:

"And again, this Gospel of the Kingdom shall be

preached in all the world, for a witness unto all nations, and then shall the end come, or the destruction of the wicked." (Writings of Joseph Smith 1:31.)

This was in fulfilment of the prophecy of Peter, who taught that the Second Coming will not occur until the "times of restitution of all things, which God hath spoken by the mouth of all his holy prophets since the world began." (Acts 3:21.)

There can be no question as to the accuracy of this verse from the King James Bible, for all other — and newer — versions confirm what it says.

The Knox Bible, produced in England by the Roman Catholic Church, reads:

"Then he will send out Jesus Christ who has now been made known unto you, but must have his dwelling place in heaven until the time when all is restored *anew*, the time which God has spoken of by his holy prophets from the beginning." (Italics added.)

The Protestant Revised Version of 1952 says: "Whom heaven must receive until the time for establishing all that God spoke by the mouths of his holy prophets from of old."

The New English Bible calls this "the time of universal restoration."

The Catholic Bible of 1947 reads exactly like the King James Version for this passage.

The American Standard Version calls this the time of the "restoration of all things"; the Rotherham Version: "the due establishment of all things"; the Twentieth Century Version: "the universal restoration"; the Weymouth Version: "the reconstitution of all things"; and all others agree.

This restoration was to be a warning to the world of the coming of the Savior — a warning of impending destruction for the unrepentant, but an assurance of hope and salvation for the righteous.

In those ancient times the Lord also made it known to John the Revelator how the gospel would be restored:

"And I saw another angel fly in the midst of heaven, having the everlasting gospel to preach unto them that dwell on the earth, and to every nation, and kindred, and tongue, and people,

"Saying with a loud voice, Fear God, and give glory to him; for the hour of his judgment is come: and worship him that made heaven, and earth, and the sea, and the fountains of waters." (Revelation 14:6-7.)

And when he gave us section 133 of the Doctrine and Covenants, he affirmed that this had (in 1831 when this revelation was given) already occurred. The angel had come eight years prior to the giving of this revelation. The Church had been organized more than a year and a half before the Lord thus spoke. So he said:

"And now, verily saith the Lord, that these things might be known among you, O inhabitants of the earth, I have sent forth mine angel flying through the midst of heaven, having the everlasting gospel, who hath appeared unto some and hath committed it unto man, who shall appear unto many that dwell on the earth.

"And this gospel shall be preached unto every nation, and kindred, and tongue, and people.

"And the servants of God shall go forth, saying with a loud voice: Fear God and give glory to him, for the hour of his judgment is come;

"And worship him that made heaven, and earth, and the sea, and the fountains of waters —

"Calling upon the name of the Lord day and night, saying: O that thou wouldst rend the heavens, that thou wouldst come down, that the mountains might flow down at thy presence.

"And it shall be answered upon their heads; for the presence of the Lord shall be as the melting fire that burneth, and as the fire which causeth the waters to boil.

"O Lord, thou shalt come down to make thy name known to thine adversaries, and all nations shall tremble at thy presence —

"When thou doest terrible things, things they look not for;

"Yea, when thou comest down, and the mountains flow

down at thy presence, thou shalt meet him who rejoiceth and worketh righteousness, who remembereth thee in thy ways.

"For since the beginning of the world have not men heard nor perceived by the ear, neither hath any eye seen, O God, besides thee, how great things thou hast prepared for him that waiteth for thee." (D&C 133:36-45.)

Even Malachi referred to this preparation by means of the gospel, to precede the Lord's coming. Said he:

"Behold, I will send my messenger, and he shall prepare the way before me: and the Lord, whom ye seek, shall suddenly come to his temple, even the messenger of the covenant, whom ye delight in: behold, he shall come, saith the Lord of hosts.

"But who may abide the day of his coming? and who shall stand when he appeareth? for he is like a refiner's fire, and like fullers' soap:

"And he shall sit as a refiner and purifier of silver: and he shall purify the sons of Levi, and purge them as gold and silver, that they may offer unto the Lord an offering in righteousness." (Malachi 3:1-3.)

Not only did this prophet speak of the messenger to prepare the way of the Lord, but he also told of still another angel who was destined to come in the latter days. He would be a different one from that described by John the Revelator, and he would have a different mission, but he would come in the great and dreadful day of the Lord as a part of this "universal restoration" of which Peter spoke.

Said Malachi in regard to this second personage:

"Behold, I will send you Elijah the prophet before the coming of the great and dreadful day of the Lord:

"And he shall turn the heart of the fathers to the children, and the heart of the children to their fathers, lest I come and smite the earth with a curse." (Malachi 4:5-6.)

Who was the messenger sent to prepare the way for the Lord's second coming? It was the Prophet Joseph Smith.

Did not the Lord say:

"Wherefore, I the Lord, knowing the calamity which should come upon the inhabitants of the earth, called upon my servant Joseph Smith, Jun., and spake unto him from heaven, and gave him commandments;

"And also gave commandments to others, that they should proclaim these things unto the world; and all this that it might be fulfilled, which was written by the prophets —

"The weak things of the world shall come forth and break down the mighty and strong ones, that man should not counsel his fellow man, neither trust in the arm of flesh —

"But that every man might speak in the name of God the Lord, even the Savior of the world;

"That faith also might increase in the earth;

"That mine everlasting covenant might be established;

"That the fulness of my gospel might be proclaimed by the weak and the simple unto the ends of the world, and before kings and rulers.

"Behold, I am God and have spoken it; these commandments are of me, and were given unto my servants in their weakness, after the manner of their language, that they might come to understanding." (D&C 1:17-24.)

As John the Baptist prepared the way before the Savior's first coming — he being a special messenger whom the Savior called the greatest prophet yet born of woman — so Joseph Smith was his latter-day messenger, preparing the way before him in this day.

Both of these great advance representatives of the Lord acted in the same capacity and in the same spirit.

Each cried out, "Repent, for the kingdom of heaven is at hand"; both declared firm testimony that Jesus is indeed the Savior and Messiah, that he is Christ the Lord.

Chapter Twenty-six

A Time of Turmoil

The second coming of the Lord will take place in a time of world convulsion. Tribulations will have been poured out upon the earth. One prediction indicated that as a result of wickedness, the earth shall be made empty "and few men left."

It was Isaiah who said:

"Behold, the Lord maketh the earth empty, amd maketh it waste, and turneth it upside down, and scattereth abroad the inhabitants thereof.

"And it shall be, as with the people, so with the priest; as with the servant, so with his master; as with the maid, so with her mistress; as with the buyer, so with the seller; as with the lender, so with the borrower; as with the taker of usury, so with the giver of usury to him.

"The land shall be utterly emptied, and utterly spoiled: for the Lord hath spoken this word.

"The earth mourneth and fadeth away, the world languisheth and fadeth away, the haughty people of the earth do languish.

"The earth also is defiled under the inhabitants thereof; because they have transgressed the laws, changed the ordinance, broken the everlasting covenant.

"Therefore hath the curse devoured the earth, and they that dwell therein are desolate: therefore the inhabitants of the earth are burned, and few men left." (Isaiah 24:1-6.)

Malachi, in describing this same period said:

"For, behold, the day cometh, that shall burn as an oven; and all the proud, yea, and all that do wickedly, shall be stubble: and the day that cometh shall burn them up, saith the Lord of hosts, that it shall leave them neither root nor branch.

"But unto you that fear my name shall the Sun of righteousness arise with healing in his wings; and ye shall go forth, and grow up as calves of the stall.

"And ye shall tread down the wicked; for they shall be ashes under the soles of your feet in the day that I shall do this, saith the Lord of hosts." (Malachi 4:1-3.)

But it is also made clear that all of these dire predictions will not be fulfilled until *after* the warning voice has come into the world.

There will be two great movements going forward simultaneously — the warning voice of the servants of God, and the pouring out of tribulations upon the wicked.

Neither will interfere with the other. The tribulations actually will accentuate the voice of the elders, and they themselves will be warnings from the Almighty.

Did not the Lord say:

"Behold, I sent you out to testify and warn the people, and it becometh every man who hath been warned to warn his neighbor.

"Therefore, they are left without excuse, and their sins are upon their own heads.

"And after your testimony cometh wrath and indignation upon the people.

"For after your testimony cometh the testimony of earthquakes, that shall cause groanings in the midst of her, and men shall fall upon the ground and shall not be able to stand.

"And also cometh the testimony of the voice of thunderings, and the voice of lightnings, and the voice of tempests, and the voice of the waves of the sea heaving themselves beyond their bounds.

"And all things shall be in commotion; and surely, men's hearts shall fail them; for fear shall come upon all people." (D&C 88:81-82, 88-91.)

The voice of warning of the elders is rapidly going forth. The gospel is now in about seventy nations, and others are being opened up as rapidly as government requirements will allow.

Eventually the truth will cover the earth as the waters cover the sea, but that will not fully come until after Christ's appearance, when barriers are thrown down, and when the elders may go freely and teach the gospel to every household in their own language.

That will be the day spoken of by the ancient prophet when every man shall "sit under his vine and under his fig tree; and none shall make them afraid: for the mouth of the Lord of hosts hath spoken it." (Micah 4:4.)

The Lord's coming will be in a time of world war and commotion. When the Lord told the Prophet Joseph Smith of these events, he said:

"And the remnant shall be gathered unto this place;

"And then they shall look for me, and, behold, I will come; and they shall see me in the clouds of heaven, clothed with power and great glory; with all the holy angels; and he that watches not for me shall be cut off.

"But before the arm of the Lord shall fall, an angel shall sound his trump, and the saints that have slept shall come forth to meet me in the cloud.

"Wherefore, if ye have slept in peace blessed are you; for as you now behold me and know that I am, even so shall ye come unto me and your souls shall live, and your redemption shall be perfected; and the saints shall come forth from the four quarters of the earth.

"Then shall the arm of the Lord fall upon the nations.

"And then shall the Lord set his foot upon this mount, and it shall cleave in twain, and the earth shall tremble, and reel to and fro, and the heavens also shall shake.

"And the Lord shall utter his voice, and all the ends of the earth shall hear it; and the nations of the earth shall mourn, and they that have laughed shall see their folly.

"And calamity shall cover the mocker, and the scorner shall be consumed; and they that have watched for iniquity shall be hewn down and cast into the fire.

"And then shall the Jews look upon me and say: What are these wounds in thine hands and in thy feet?

"Then shall they know that I am the Lord; for I will say unto them: These wounds are the wounds with which I was wounded in the house of my friends. I am he who was lifted up. I am Jesus that was crucified. I am the Son of God.

"And then shall they weep because of their iniquities; then shall they lament because they persecuted their king." (D&C 45:43-53.)

Zechariah speaks of this same event as follows:

"For I will gather all nations against Jerusalem to battle; and the city shall be taken, and the houses rifled, and the women ravished; and half of the city shall go forth into captivity, and the residue of the people shall not be cut off from the city.

"Then shall the Lord go forth, and fight against those nations, as when he fought in the day of battle.

"And his feet shall stand in that day upon the mount of Olives, which is before Jerusalem on the east, and the mount of Olives shall cleave in the midst thereof toward the east and toward the west, and there shall be a very great valley; and half of the mountain shall remove toward the north, and half of it toward the south.

"And ye shall flee to the valley of the mountains; for the valley of the mountains shall reach unto Azal: yea, ye shall flee, like as ye fled from before the earthquake in the days of Uzziah king of Judah: and the Lord my God shall come, and all the saints with thee.

"And it shall come to pass in that day, that the light shall not be clear, nor dark:

"But it shall be one day which shall be known to the Lord, not day, nor night: but it shall come to pass, that at evening time it shall be light." (Zechariah 14:2-7.)

He also said this in a previous chapter:

"And it shall come to pass in that day, saith the Lord of hosts that I will cut off the names of the idols out of the land,

and they shall no more be remembered: and also I will cause the prophets and the unclean spirit to pass out of the land.

"And it shall come to pass, that when any shall yet prophesy, then his father and his mother that begat him shall say unto him, Thou shalt not live; for thou speakest lies in the name of the Lord: and his father and his mother that begat him shall thrust him through when he prophesieth.

"And it shall come to pass in that day, that the prophets shall be ashamed every one of his vision, when he hath prophesied; neither shall they wear a rough garment to deceive:

"But he shall say, I am no prophet, I am an husbandman; for man taught me to keep cattle from my youth.

"And one shall say unto him, What are these wounds in thine hands? Then he shall answer, Those with which I was wounded in the house of my friends.

"Awake, O sword, against my shepherd, and against the man that is my fellow, saith the Lord of hosts: smite the shepherd, and the sheep shall be scattered: and I will turn mine hand upon the little ones.

"And it shall come to pass that in all the land, saith the Lord, two parts therein shall be cut off and die; but the third shall be left therein.

"And I will bring the third part through the fire, and will refine them as silver is refined, and will try them as gold is tried: they shall call on my name, and I will hear them: I will say, It is my people: and they shall say, The Lord is my God." (Zechariah 13:2-9.)

This prophet says something else of great interest regarding Jerusalem:

"Behold, I will make Jerusalem a cup of trembling unto all the people round about, when they shall be in the siege both against Judah and against Jerusalem.

"And in that day will I make Jerusalem a burdensome stone for all people: all that burden themselves with it shall be cut in pieces, though all the people of the earth be gathered together against it." (Zechariah 12:2-3.)

It seems that all nations will be gathered at Jerusalem to battle just prior to the Lord's coming. (See Zechariah 14:2.)

Ezekiel gives further details about this last great war prior to the Lord's appearance:

"Therefore, son of man, prophesy and say unto Gog, Thus saith the Lord God; In that day when my people of Israel dwelleth safely, shall thou not know it?

"And thou shalt come from thy place out of the north parts, thou, and many people with thee, all of them riding upon horses, a great company, and a mighty army:

"And thou shalt come up against my people of Israel, as a cloud to cover the land; it shall be in the latter days, and I will bring thee against my land, that the heathen may know me, when I shall be sanctified in thee, O Gog, before their eyes.

"Thus saith the Lord God; Art thou he of whom I have spoken in old time by my servants the prophets of Israel, which prophesied in those days many years that I would bring thee against them?

"And it shall come to pass at the same time when Gog shall come against the land of Israel, saith the Lord God, that my fury shall come up in my face.

"For in my jealousy and in the fire of my wrath have I spoken, Surely in that day there shall be a great shaking in the land of Israel:

"So that the fishes of the sea, and the fowls of the heaven, and the beasts of the field, and all creeping things that creep upon the earth, and all the men that are upon the face of the earth, shall shake at my presence, and the mountains shall be thrown down, and the steep places shall fall, and every wall shall fall to the ground.

"And I will call for a sword against him throughout all my mountains, saith the Lord God: every man's sword shall be against his brother.

"And I will plead against him with pestilence and with blood; and I will rain upon him, and upon his bands, and upon the many people that are with him, an overflowing rain and great hailstones, fire, and brimstone.

"Thus will I magnify myself, and sanctify myself; and I will be known in the eyes of many nations, and they shall know that I am the Lord." (Ezekiel 38:14-23.)

The destruction will be so great that "seven months shall

the house of Israel be burying of them, that they may cleanse the land.

"Yea, all the people of the land shall bury them; and it shall be to them a renown the day that I shall be glorified, saith the Lord God.

"And they shall sever out men of continual employment, passing through the land to bury with the passengers those that remain upon the face of the earth, to cleanse it: after the end of seven months shall they search." (Ezekiel 39:12-14.)

Zechariah then goes on to say:

"The Lord also shall save the tents of Judah first, that the glory of the house of David and the glory of the inhabitants of Jerusalem do not magnify themselves against Judah.

"In that day shall the Lord defend the inhabitants of Jerusalem; and he that is feeble among them at that day shall be as David; and the house of David shall be as God, as the angel of the Lord before them.

"And it shall come to pass in that day, that I will seek to destroy all the nations that come against Jerusalem.

"And I will pour upon the house of David, and upon the inhabitants of Jerusalem, the spirit of grace and of supplications: and they shall look upon me whom they have pierced, and they shall mourn for him, as one mourneth for his only son, and shall be in bitterness for him, as one that is in bitterness for his firstborn.

"In that day shall there be a great mourning in Jerusalem, as the mourning of Hadadrimmon in the valley of Megiddon.

"And the land shall mourn, every family apart; the family of the house of David apart, and their wives apart; the family of the house of Nathan apart, and their wives apart;

"The family of the house of Levi apart, and their wives apart; the family of Shimei apart, and their wives apart;

"All the families that remain, every family apart, and their wives apart." (Zechariah 12:7-14.)

In modern revelation the Lord said:

"And except those days should be shortened, there should none of their flesh be saved; but for the elect's sake, according to the covenant, those days shall be shortened.

"Behold, these things I have spoken unto you concerning the Jews; and again, after the tribulation of those days which shall come upon Jerusalem, if any man shall say unto you, Lo, here is Christ, or there, believe him not;

"For in those days there shall also arise false Christs, and false prophets, and shall show great signs and wonders, insomuch, that, if possible, they shall deceive the very elect, who are the elect according to the covenant.

"Behold, I speak these things unto you for the elect's sake; and you also shall hear of wars, and rumors of wars; see that ye be not troubled, for all I have told you must come to pass; but the end is not yet." (Writings of Joseph Smith 1:20-23.)

When shall these things be? The Lord said:

"But of that day, and hour, no one knoweth; no, not the angels of God in heaven, but my Father only.

"But as it was in the days of Noah, so it shall be also at the coming of the Son of Man;

"For it shall be with them, as it was in the days which were before the flood; for until the day that Noah entered into the ark they were eating and drinking, marrying and giving in marriage;

"And knew not until the flood came, and took them all away; so shall also the coming of the Son of Man be.

"Then shall be fulfilled that which is written, that in the last days, two shall be in the field, the one shall be taken, and the other left;

"Two shall be grinding at the mill, the one shall be taken, and the other left;

"And what I say unto one, I say unto all men; watch, therefore, for you know not at what hour your Lord doth come.

"But know this, if the good man of the house had known in what watch the thief would come, he would have watched, and would not have suffered his house to have been broken up, but would have been ready.

"Therefore be ye also ready, for in such an hour as ye think not, the Son of Man cometh.

"Who, then, is a faithful and wise servant, whom his lord hath made ruler over his household, to give them meat in due season?

"Blessed is that servant whom his lord, when he cometh, shall find so doing; and verily I say unto you, he shall make him ruler over all his goods.

"But if that evil servant shall say in his heart: My lord delayeth his coming,

"And shall begin to smite his fellow-servants, and to eat and drink with the drunken,

"The lord of that servant shall come in a day when he looketh not for him, and in an hour that he is not aware of,

"And shall cut him asunder, and shall appoint him his portion with the hypocrites; there shall be weeping and gnashing of teeth.

"And thus cometh the end of the wicked, according to the prophecy of Moses, saying: They shall be cut off from among the people; but the end of the earth is not yet, but by and by." (Writings of Joseph Smith 1:40-50.)

Joel spoke of these days also when he said:

"Proclaim ye this among the Gentiles; Prepare war, wake up the mighty men, let all the men of war draw near; let them come up:

"Beat your plowshares into swords, and your pruning-hooks into spears: let the weak say, I am strong.

"Assemble yourselves, and come, all ye heathen, and gather yourselves together round about: thither cause thy mighty ones to come down, O Lord.

"Let the heathen be wakened, and come up to the valley of Jehoshaphat: for there will I sit to judge all the heathen round about.

"Put ye in the sickle, for the harvest is ripe: come, get you down; for the press is full, the fats overflow; for their wickedness is great.

"Multitudes, multitudes in the valley of decision: for the day of the Lord is near in the valley of decision.

"The sun and the moon shall be darkened, and the stars shall withdraw their shining.

"The Lord also shall roar out of Zion, and utter his voice

from Jerusalem; and the heavens and the earth shall shake: but the Lord will be the hope of his people, and the strength of the children of Israel.

"So shall ye know that I am the Lord your God dwelling in Zion, my holy mountain: then shall Jerusalem be holy, and there shall no strangers pass through her any more.

"And it shall come to pass in that day, that the mountains shall drop down new wine, and the hills shall flow with milk, and all the rivers of Judah shall flow with waters, and a fountain shall come forth of the house of the Lord, and shall water the valley of Shittim.

"Egypt shall be a desolation, and Edom shall be a desolate wilderness, for the violence against the children of Judah, because they have shed innocent blood in their land.

"But Judah shall dwell for ever, and Jerusalem from generation to generation.

"For I will cleanse their blood that I have not cleansed: for the Lord dwelleth in Zion." (Joel 3:9-21.)

As the prophet indicated, the Lord shall come in the midst of the great war, and the Jews shall recognize him as their Messiah, and then redemption will come to them.

And as the Lord said to Joseph Smith: "They also of the tribe of Judah, after their pain shall be sanctified in holiness before the Lord, to dwell in his presence day and night, forever and ever." (D&C 133:35.)

An interesting passage in connection with the Second Coming is this:

"And it shall be said: Who is this that cometh down from God in heaven with dyed garments; yea, from the regions which are not known, clothed in his glorious apparel, traveling in the greatness of his strength?

"And he shall say: I am he who spake in righteousness, mighty to save.

"And the Lord shall be red in his apparel, and his garments like him that treadeth in the wine-vat.

"And so great shall be the glory of his presence that the sun shall hide his face in shame, and the moon shall withhold its light, and the stars shall be hurled from their places.

"And his voice shall be heard: I have trodden the wine-press alone, and have brought judgment upon all people; and none were with me;

"And I have trampled them in my fury, and I did tread upon them in mine anger, and their blood have I sprinkled upon my garments, and stained all my raiment; for this was the day of vengeance which was in my heart.

"And now the year of my redeemed is come; and they shall mention the loving kindness of their Lord, and all that he has bestowed upon them according to his goodness, and according to his loving kindness, forever and ever.

"In all their afflictions he was afflicted. And the angel of his presence saved them; and in his love, and in his pity, he redeemed them, and bore them, and carried them all the days of old;

"Yea, and Enoch also, and they who were with him; the prophets who were before him; and Noah also, and they who were before him; and Moses also, and they who were before him;

"And from Moses to Elijah, and from Elijah to John, who were with Christ in his resurrection, and the holy apostles, with Abraham, Isaac, and Jacob, shall be in the presence of the Lamb.

"And the graves of the saints shall be opened; and they shall come forth and stand on the right hand of the Lamb, when he shall stand upon Mount Zion, and upon the holy city, the New Jerusalem; and they shall sing the song of the Lamb, day and night forever and ever.

"And for this cause, that men might be made partakers of the glories which were to be revealed, the Lord sent forth the fulness of his gospel, his everlasting covenant, reasoning in plainness and simplicity —

"To prepare the weak for those things which are coming on the earth, and for the Lord's errand in the day when the weak shall confound the wise, and the little one become a strong nation, and two shall put their tens of thousands to flight.

"And by the weak things of the earth the Lord shall thrash the nations by the power of his Spirit.

"And for this cause these commandments were given; they were commanded to be kept from the world in the day that they were given, but now are to go forth unto all flesh —

"And this according to the mind and will of the Lord, who ruleth over all flesh.

"And unto him that repenteth and sanctifieth himself before the Lord shall be given eternal life.

"And upon them that hearken not to the voice of the Lord shall be fulfilled that which was written by the prophet Moses, that they should be cut off from among the people.

"And also that which was written by the prophet Malachi: For, behold, the day cometh that shall burn as an oven, and all the proud, yea, and all that do wickedly, shall be stubble; and the day that cometh shall burn them up, saith the Lord of hosts, that it shall leave them neither root nor branch.

"Wherefore, this shall be the answer of the Lord unto them:

"In that day when I came unto mine own, no man among you received me, and you were driven out.

"When I called again there was none of you to answer; yet my arm was not shortened at all that I could not redeem, neither my power to deliver.

"Behold, at my rebuke I dry up the sea. I make the rivers a wilderness; their fish stink, and die for thirst.

"I clothe the heavens with blackness, and make sackcloth their covering.

"And this shall ye have of my hand — ye shall lie down in sorrow.

"Behold, and lo, there are none to deliver you; for ye obeyed not my voice when I called to you out of the heavens; ye believed not my servants, and when they were sent unto you ye received them not.

"Wherefore, they sealed up the testimony and bound up the law, and ye were delivered over unto darkness.

"These shall go away into outer darkness, where there is weeping, and wailing, and gnashing of teeth.

"Behold the Lord your God hath spoken it. Amen." (D&C 133:46-74.)

That the Savior will appear in other places besides Jerusalem is indicated as follows:

"For behold, the Lord God hath sent forth the angel crying through the midst of heaven, saying: Prepare ye the way of the Lord, and make his paths straight, for the hour of his coming is nigh —

"When the Lamb shall stand upon Mount Zion, and with him a hundred and forty-four thousand, having his Father's name written on their foreheads.

"Wherefore, prepare ye for the coming of the Bridegroom; go ye, go out to meet him.

"For behold, he shall stand upon the mount of Olivet, and upon the mighty ocean, even the great deep, and upon the islands of the sea, and upon the land of Zion.

"And he shall utter his voice out of Zion, and he shall speak from Jerusalem, and his voice shall be heard among all people;

"And it shall be a voice as the voice of many waters, and as the voice of a great thunder, which shall break down the mountains, and the valleys shall not be found." (D&C 133:17-22.)

Another significant event will be the alteration of the face of the earth. Said the Lord:

"He shall command the great deep, and it shall be driven back into the north countries, and the islands shall become one land;

"And the land of Jerusalem and the land of Zion shall be turned back into their own place, and the earth shall be like as it was in the days before it was divided." (D&C 133:23-24; see also Genesis 10:25.)

Chapter Twenty-seven

America's Part

Great events will take place in America related to and including the glorious second coming of the Lord.

America is the land of Zion, choice above all other lands.

America is that place where — in the tops of its mountains — prophets said the house of the Lord would be established in the last days, and to which all nations will flow.

America is the place — in its very heartland — where the New Jerusalem will be built, the modern City of Zion, where the great temple of latter days will rise, to which the Lord will come.

America is the land of the Ancient of Days, where Adam once gathered together his posterity while he was still in mortality, and where again he will yet assemble the mighty servants of the Lord, then to turn over his stewardship to the Savior of all mankind.

America is that land from whence the law of the Lord will go to all the world, as the word of the Lord will go out from Jerusalem. (See Isaiah 2:3.)

America will be the place to which the Savior will come with the hosts of heaven as he opens his millennial reign. And who shall say that America will not be the place for the throne of Jesus as he reigns for a thousand years in righteousness and peace here upon his footstool?

As a prophet of old looked down the centuries and saw this day, he said:

"Wherefore, the remnant of the house of Joseph shall be built upon this land; and it shall be a land of their inheritance; and they shall build up a holy city unto the Lord, like unto the Jerusalem of old; and they shall no more be confounded, until the end come when the earth shall pass away." (Ether 13:4-8.)

Jesus himself said to the Nephites:

"Behold, this people will I establish in this land, unto the fulfilling of the covenant which I made with your father Jacob; and it shall be a New Jerusalem. And the powers of heaven shall be in the midst of this people; yea, even I will be in the midst of you." (3 Nephi 20:22.)

As Isaiah indicates, there will be two world capitals during the reign of Jesus upon the earth. One will be the old Jerusalem in Palestine, the other will be the New Jerusalem, or Zion, in America. "Out of Zion shall go forth the law, and the word of the Lord from Jerusalem." (Isaiah 2:3.)

The Prophet Joseph said:

"Now we learn from the Book of Mormon the very identical continent and spot of land upon which the New Jerusalem is to stand, and it must be caught up according to the vision of John upon the isle of Patmos.

"Now many will feel disposed to say, that this New Jerusalem spoken of, is the Jerusalem that was built by the Jews on the eastern continent. But you will see, from Revelation xxi:2, there was a New Jerusalem coming down from God out of heaven, adorned as a bride for her husband; that after this, the Revelator was caught away in the Spirit, to a great and high mountain, and saw the great and holy city descending out of heaven from God. Now there are two cities spoken of here. As everything cannot be had in so narrow a compass as a letter, I shall say with brevity, that there is a New Jerusalem to be established on this continent, and also Jerusalem shall be rebuilt on the eastern continent (see Book of Mormon, Ether xiii:1-12). 'Behold, Ether saw the days of Christ, and he spake also concerning the house of Israel, and the Jerusalem from whence Lehi should come; after it should be destroyed, it should be built up again, a holy city unto the Lord, wherefore it could not be a New Jerusalem, for it had been in a time of old.' '' (Joseph Fielding Smith, comp., *Teachings of the Prophet Joseph Smith* [Salt Lake City: Deseret Book Company, 1977], pp. 85-86: hereafter cited as *TPJS*.)

The Prophet Joseph also said:

"The city of Zion spoken of by David, in the one hundred and second Psalm, will be built upon the land of America, 'And the ransomed of the Lord shall return, and come to Zion with songs and everlasting joy upon their heads.' (Isaiah xxxv:10); and then they will be delivered from the overflowing scourge that shall pass through the land. But Judah shall obtain deliverance at Jerusalem. See Joel ii:32; Isaiah xxvi:20 and 21; Jeremiah xxxi:12; Psalms 1:5; Ezekiel xxxiv:11, 12 and 13. These are testimonies that the Good Shepherd will put forth His own sheep, and lead them out from all nations where they have been scattered in a cloudy and dark day, to Zion, and to Jerusalem; besides many more testimonies which might be brought." (*TPJS*, p. 17.)

With respect to the old Jerusalem, the Prophet Joseph said:

"Judah must return, Jerusalem must be rebuilt, and the temple, and water come out from under the temple, and the waters of the Dead Sea be healed. It will take some time to rebuild the walls of the city and the temple, &c.; and all this must be done before the Son of Man will make His appearance. There will be wars and rumors of wars, signs in the heavens above and on the earth beneath, the sun turned into darkness and the moon to blood, earthquakes in divers places, the seas heaving beyond their bounds; then will appear one grand sign of the Son of Man in heaven. But what will the world do? They will say it is a planet, a comet, etc. But the Son of Man will come as the sign of the coming of the Son of Man, which will be as the light of the morning cometh out of the east." (*TPJS*, pp. 286-287.)

James E. Talmage, speaking of the New Jerusalem to be erected in America, also refers to the City of Enoch which was taken into heaven and says that eventually the two cities will become one. This is not said in reference to the old Jerusalem in Palestine, but to the New Jerusalem in America and the City of Enoch. Says he:

"Great events are to mark the latter days; the elect are to be gathered from the four quarters of the earth to a place prepared for them; the tabernacle of the Lord is to be established there, and the place 'shall be called Zion, a New Jerusalem.' Then Enoch and his people are to return to earth and meet the gathered elect in the holy place.

"We have seen that the names Zion and New Jerusalem are used interchangeably; and, furthermore, that righteous people as well as sanctified places are called Zion; for, by the Lord's special word, Zion to Him means 'the pure in heart.' The Church in this day teaches that the New Jerusalem seen by John and by the prophet Ether, as descending from the heavens in glory, is the return of exalted Enoch and his righteous people; and that the people or Zion of Enoch, and the modern Zion, or the gathered saints on the western continent, will become one people." (James E. Talmage, *The Articles of Faith* [Salt Lake City: The Church of Jesus Christ of Latter-day Saints, 1977], pp. 351-352.)

When the Saints of Joseph Smith's day learned through his revelations that the City of Zion was to be established in America, they of course asked about its location. Joseph also wished to know. But the Lord did not reveal it immediately.

Later he made it known that the city was to be built in Jackson County, Missouri, and he instructed the Prophet to begin gathering the Saints to that place.

Not far from the center of the city of Independence, the Lord designated the site on which the great temple of latter days will be built. The site was formally dedicated.

Although the Lord urged his people to begin construction of the City of Zion in that day, they were not humble and faithful enough to do so, and as a result, the Lord allowed the mobs to drive them out. When the Prophet, in great disappointment, asked the Lord why this had taken place, he received this revelation:

"I, the Lord, have suffered the affliction to come upon

them, wherewith they have been afflicted, in consequence of their transgressions;

"Yet I will own them, and they shall be mine in that day when I shall come to make up my jewels.

"Therefore, they must needs be chastened and tried, even as Abraham, who was commanded to offer up his only son.

"For all those who will not endure chastening, but deny me, cannot be sanctified.

"Behold, I say unto you, there were jarrings, and contentions, and envyings, and strifes, and lustful and covetous desires among them; therefore by these things they polluted their inheritances.

"They were slow to hearken unto the voice of the Lord their God; therefore, the Lord their God is slow to hearken unto their prayers, to answer them in the day of their trouble.

"In the day of their peace they esteemed lightly my counsel; but, in the day of their trouble, of necessity they feel after me.

"Verily I say unto you, notwithstanding their sins, my bowels are filled with compassion towards them. I will not utterly cast them off; and in the day of wrath I will remember mercy." (D&C 101:2-9.)

But the Lord assured his people in this same revelation that although he now postponed the time of building that city, it would yet be built, and would not be "moved out of her place." (D&C 101:17.) The location would remain the same, for "there is none other place appointed than that which I have appointed; neither shall there be." (D&C 101:20; see also D&C 105:1-13.)

When Zion eventually is built in Missouri, the scriptures indicate that the Lamanites will have an important part in its construction. The Savior mentioned this to the Nephites as he discoursed about the gentiles who were to occupy this land of America, and by whom the gospel would be carried abroad. He said that if the gentiles "will repent and hearken unto my words, and harden not their hearts, I will establish my church among them, and they shall come in unto the covenant and be numbered among this the remnant of Jacob, unto whom I have given this land for their inheritance;

"And they shall assist my people, the remnant of Jacob, and also as many of the house of Israel as shall come, that they may build a city, which shall be called the New Jerusalem.

"And then shall they assist my people that they may be gathered in, who are scattered upon all the face of the land, in unto the New Jerusalem.

"And then shall the power of heaven come down among them; and I also will be in the midst." (3 Nephi 21:22-25.)

There is significance also to the words of Ether, who "saw the days of Christ, and he spake concerning a New Jerusalem upon this land; . . .

"And that a New Jerusalem should be built up upon this land, unto the remnant of the seed of Joseph." (Ether 13:4-6.)

Chapter Twenty-eight

"I Am the Resurrection"

Lazarus, a close friend of Jesus in mortality, became sick and died.

The regret of Mary and Martha, sisters of Lazarus, was that the Savior had not arrived in Bethany soon enough to heal him before he passed away.

It was with this thought that Martha greeted the Lord when he came to their home: "Lord, if thou hadst been here, my brother had not died."

This was the measure of her great trust in Jesus. She added to this expression of faith as she continued: "But I know, that even now, whatsoever thou wilt ask of God, God will give it thee."

Comforting her, Jesus said, "Thy brother shall rise again."

Martha responded, "I know that he shall rise again in the resurrection at the last day."

Jesus said to her: "I am the resurrection, and the life." (John 11:21-25.)

As the Source of life, he planned no cessation of it. Life is eternal, it goes on forever, it can never end. He is eternal, and as he never ends, so life never ends. It is forever, just as Jesus is forever.

In the economy of God, life has continuous, unending purpose. That purpose is that we may become like God. When he says there is no death, he speaks the truth if we think of death as the termination of existence. Existence is forever.

As the architect of our being, the Lord planned each major step of our journey from eternity to eternity.

Before the world was ever made, we lived in a joyful preexistent life. The purpose of the creation of our earth was that it should become a home for us. To live here we must become mortal, which meant achieving this step by the process of birth. This God also planned.

Upon finishing our course of schooling here in mortality, there must be a means of leaving it; this also the Lord provided. It was death, a door through which we pass into the next stage of our careers. This again was all planned by the Lord.

After a waiting period in the world of departed spirits, the Lord devised the final step in this process. It was to reunite the spirit and the body in a manner which would be everlasting. That was called resurrection. God planned it also.

Of the Creation the Father said, "By the word of my power, have I created them, which is mine Only Begotten Son, who is full of grace and truth.

"And worlds without number have I created; and I also created them for mine own purpose; and by the Son I created them, which is mine Only Begotten." (Moses 1:32-33.)

And why? "To bring to pass the immortality and eternal life of man." (Moses 1:39.)

In the Sermon on the Mount the Savior expressed this intent in the form of a commandment when he said: "Be ye therefore perfect, even as your Father which is in heaven is perfect." (Matthew 5:48.)

As children of God, then, our purpose is to become like him. That is the meaning of bringing to pass our immortality and eternal life. That is the reason for our steps from preexistence to mortality, from mortality to the world of departed spirits, which comes immediately after death, and from the world of departed spirits to resurrection.

This was all part of the original eternal plan. It was devised from the very beginning. The Father and the Son labored together in the entire matter, the Father working through the Son, and giving to the Son all power in heaven and in earth.

So the Son became Creator and Savior of all mankind, conqueror of death, author of the Resurrection and the first fruits of them that slept.

So he could well say to Martha: "I am the resurrection and the life."

His own resurrection was a physical one. He could eat as he did in mortality. He invited people to "handle me, and see; for a spirit hath not flesh and bones, as ye see me have." (Luke 24:39.)

He allowed twenty-five hundred Nephites to examine the scars in his body, as proof of his crucifixion and resurrection, and to give full assurance to those wondering people that he was indeed the Christ. (See 3 Nephi 11:13-17.)

"The Father has a body . . . as tangible as man's; the Son also," said the Prophet Joseph Smith. (D&C 130:22.)

Christ became like his Father, requiring the physical resurrection of which we have testimony. We, too, are to become like our Father. We, too, then, must have a physical resurrection.

The prophet Alma explained that "it meaneth the reuniting of the soul with the body" (Alma 40:18), and then he said further:

"The soul shall be restored to the body, and the body to the soul; yea, and every limb and joint shall be restored to its body; yea, even a hair of the head shall not be lost; but all things shall be restored to their proper and perfect frame." (Alma 40:23.)

This is not a temporary matter. This reuniting of spirit and body is to be eternal, for as Alma also wrote:

"They can die no more; their spirits uniting with their bodies, never to be divided; thus the whole becoming spiritual and immortal, that they can no more see corruption." (Alma 11:45.)

In giving us what is now section 88 of the Doctrine and Covenants, the Lord explained that we will have the same bodies we have here in mortality, saying that we "shall receive the same body which was a natural body; even ye shall receive your bodies, and your glory shall be that glory by which your bodies are quickened." (D&C 88:28.)

All will be raised. Paul said, "As in Adam all die, even so in Christ shall all be made alive." (1 Corinthians 15:22.)

There are to be gradations of glory, but even the wicked will be raised from their graves. They had no voice in Adam's fall; they have no voice as to coming forth from the tomb.

Where they do have decision, however, is in their present obedience or disobedience to the gospel, for their resurrected glory shall be according to their works. (See D&C 88;76.)

But all are raised by the Savior, who broke the bands of death. He spoke truly when he said: "I am the resurrection and the life."

Chapter Twenty-nine

Alpha and Omega

Even before the Church was organized, Jesus identified himself clearly and distinctly to the Prophet Joseph Smith and Martin Harris when he said:

"I am Alpha and Omega, Christ the Lord; yea, even I am he, the beginning and the end, the Redeemer of the world."

He then went on to say:

"I, having accomplished and finished the will of him whose I am, even the Father, concerning me — having done this that I might subdue all things unto myself —

"Retaining all power, even to the destroying of Satan and his works at the end of the world, and the last great day of judgment, which I shall pass upon the inhabitants thereof, judging every man according to his works and the deeds which he hath done." (D&C 19:1-3.)

He is the Creator of heaven and earth; he is the Author of our faith. He finished his atonement in Gethsemane and on the cross, broke the bands of death in the Resurrection, and paid the price for the sins of all mankind, so that they may not suffer if they would repent. (See D&C 19:15-19.)

The Atonement was completed; resurrection was assured to us all, and the way was opened whereby we may become "perfect, even as your Father which is in heaven is perfect" (Matthew 5:48), if we will but accept it and live it.

As he expired on the cross, he cried out, "It is finished," and so it was.

The task was difficult. Only an Infinite Personage could accomplish it. But he was infinite. He was divine; he was Deity, even as his Father.

The suffering he endured "caused myself, even God, the greatest of all, to tremble because of pain, and to bleed at every pore, and to suffer both body and spirit." (D&C 19:18.)

For an infinite number of sins committed by an infinite number of wayward humans, an infinite price had to be paid. Only Deity could pay that price, and Jesus did.

So he was the author and finisher of our faith, as the apostle Paul wrote to the Hebrews:

"Let us lay aside every weight, and the sin which doth so easily beset us, and let us run with patience the race that is set before us,

"Looking unto Jesus the author and finisher of our faith; who for the joy that was set before him endured the cross, despising the shame, and is set down at the right hand of the throne of God." (Hebrews 12:1-2.)

He holds out to us his everlasting promise of salvation if we will but serve him. He would gather us, even as a hen gathereth her chickens, and he extends this gracious invitation:

"Come unto me, all ye that labour and are heavy laden, and I will give you rest.

"Take my yoke upon you, and learn of me; for I am meek and lowly in heart: and ye shall find rest unto your souls.

"For my yoke is easy, and my burden is light." (Matthew 11:28-30. Italics added.)

Can we refuse such an invitation?

Chapter Thirty

We May See Him

Verily, thus saith the Lord: It shall come to pass that every soul who forsaketh his sins and cometh unto me, and calleth on my name, and obeyeth my voice, and keepeth my commandments, shall see my face and know that I am;

"And that I am the true light that lighteth every man that cometh into the world;

"And that I am in the Father, and the Father in me, and the Father and I are one —

"The Father because he gave me of his fulness, and the Son because I was in the world and made flesh my tabernacle, and dwelt among the sons of men.

"I was in the world and received of my Father, and the works of him were plainly manifest.

"And John saw and bore record of the fulness of my glory, and the fulness of John's record is hereafter to be revealed.

"And he bore record, saying: I saw his glory, that he was in the beginning, before the world was;

"Therefore, in the beginning the Word was, for he was the Word, even the messenger of salvation —

"The light and the Redeemer of the world; the Spirit of

truth, who came into the world, because the world was made by him, and in him was the life of men and the light of men.

"The worlds were made by him; men were made by him; all things were made by him, and through him, and of him.

"And I, John, bear record that I beheld his glory, as the glory of the Only Begotten of the Father, full of grace and truth, even the Spirit of truth, which came and dwelt in the flesh, and dwelt among us.

"And I, John, saw that he received not of the fulness at the first, but received grace for grace;

"And he received not of the fulness at first, but continued from grace to grace, until he received a fulness;

"And thus he was called the Son of God, because he received not of the fulness at the first.

"And I, John, bear record, and lo, the heavens were opened, and the Holy Ghost descended upon him in the form of a dove, and sat upon him, and there came a voice out of heaven saying: This is my beloved Son.

"And I, John, bear record that he received a fulness of the glory of the Father;

"And he received all power, both in heaven and on earth, and the glory of the Father was with him, for he dwelt in him.

"And it shall come to pass, that if you are faithful you shall receive the fulness of the record of John.

"I give unto you these sayings that you may understand and know how to worship, and know what you worship, that you may come unto the Father in my name, and in due time receive of his fulness.

"For if you keep my commandments you shall receive of his fulness, and be glorified in me as I am in the Father; therefore, I say unto you, you shall receive grace for grace." (D&C 93:1-20.)

Index